DREAMS

God is releasing to us prophetic revelation in these last days, and Jane Hamon offers clear, biblical, practical teaching on how to understand and interpret our dreams. This book is a great tool for encouraging, equipping and releasing an army of Daniels and Josephs who can encourage leaders and change nations!

Ché Ahn

SENIOR PASTOR, HARVEST ROCK CHURCH
PRESIDENT, HARVEST INTERNATIONAL MINISTRIES
PASADENA, CALIFORNIA

I gleaned so much from Jane Hamon's insight and instruction. Her book is based on Scripture and shows how important dreams are to the person who loves our Lord, Jesus Christ. *Dreams and Visions* is well worth the time to read.

Bobbye Byerly

WORLD PRAYER CENTER
MOBILIZATION AND TRAINER OF INTERCESSORS
COLORADO SPRINGS, COLORADO

Jane Hamon's down-to-earth style, combined with her profound scriptural insights and personal experiences, sheds a refreshing new light on this important subject. I treasure my copy of *Dreams and Visions* and will refer to it often in my quest to understand God and help His people.

David Cannistraci

PASTOR, EVANGEL CHRISTIAN FELLOWSHIP
SAN JOSE, CALIFORNIA

This is a fascinating book! If you dream,
you need to read *Dreams and Visions*.

Cindy Jacobs

AUTHOR OF *THE VOICE OF GOD* AND *WOMEN OF DESTINY*
COFOUNDER, GENERALS OF INTERCESSION
COLORADO SPRINGS, COLORADO

It is indeed rewarding to see these timely, scriptural truths being
clearly taught in *Dreams and Visions*. I heard Jane Hamon teach on this
subject and was deeply impressed. She has done her homework and
teaches both in a scholarly and experiential way.

Fuchsia T. Pickett

AUTHOR OF *THE NEXT MOVE OF GOD*
BLOUNTVILLE, TENNESSEE

In our busy world, many times we fail to slow down and
communicate with a holy God. So, in the quiet of the night,
He communicates to us. *Dreams and Visions* is a key book for this
time. God is communicating to His people, and we must learn
to interpret what He is saying!

Chuck D. Pierce

AUTHOR OF *POSSESSING YOUR INHERITANCE*
PRESIDENT, GLORY OF ZION INTERNATIONAL
COLORADO SPRINGS, COLORADO

I frequently find myself a bit edgy when people begin telling me about their dreams and visions, partly because I have observed more than enough naiveté and superficiality when the subject comes up. Now maybe things will be different. Jane Hamon skillfully and sensitively dispels the fog surrounding the issue of our dreams with insightful biblical information combined with personal experience. Do not miss this book!

C. Peter Wagner
CHANCELLOR, WAGNER LEADERSHIP INSTITUTE
COLORADO SPRINGS, COLORADO

God communicates to His people today, but many times He is missed or misunderstood. Jane Hamon brings remarkable clarity to a frequent form of God's communication in her book. I love the very practical and scriptural way Jane addresses the topic. *Dreams and Visions* is a must for all who desire to clearly hear the voice of the Lord.

Barbara Wentroble
AUTHOR OF *PROPHETIC INTERCESSION* AND *A PEOPLE OF DESTINY*
DUNCANVILLE, TEXAS

UNDERSTANDING YOUR DREAMS AND
HOW GOD CAN USE THEM TO SPEAK TO YOU TODAY

DREAMS
AND
VISIONS

JANE HAMON

Regal

A Division of Gospel Light
Ventura, California, U.S.A.

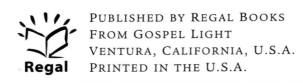

PUBLISHED BY REGAL BOOKS
FROM GOSPEL LIGHT
VENTURA, CALIFORNIA, U.S.A.
PRINTED IN THE U.S.A.

Regal Books is a ministry of Gospel Light, a Christian publisher dedicated to serving the local church. We believe God's vision for Gospel Light is to provide church leaders with biblical, user-friendly materials that will help them evangelize, disciple and minister to children, youth and families.

It is our prayer that this Regal book will help you discover biblical truth for your own life and help you meet the needs of others. May God richly bless you.

For a free catalog of resources from Regal Books/Gospel Light, please call your Christian supplier or contact us at 1-800-4-GOSPEL *or* www.regalbooks.com.

Dreams and Visions was originally published by Christian International Ministries Network in 1997.

Cover Design by Kevin Keller
Interior Design by Robert Williams
Edited by David Webb

Library of Congress Cataloging-in-Publication Data
Hamon, Jane, 1961—
    Dreams and visions / Jane Hamon.
        p.   cm.
    Includes bibliographical references.
    ISBN 0-8307-2569-5 (trade pbk.)
    1. Dreams—Religious aspects—Christianity. 2. Visions. I. Title.

BR115.D74 H35 2000
248.2'9—dc21   00-027220

8 9 10 11 12 13 14 15 16 17 18 19 / 12 11 10 09 08 07 06 05 04

Rights for publishing this book in other languages are contracted by Gospel Light Worldwide, the international nonprofit ministry of Gospel Light. Gospel Light Worldwide also provides publishing and technical assistance to international publishers dedicated to producing Sunday School and Vacation Bible School curricula and books in the languages of the world. For additional information, visit www.gospellightworldwide.org; write to Gospel Light Worldwide, P.O. Box 3875, Ventura, CA 93006; or send an e-mail to info@gospellightworldwide.org.

This book is dedicated to my family: my husband, Tom—the man of my dreams—and my three wonderful children, Crystal, Tiffany and Jason.

Tom, your constant love and continuous support have encouraged me to grow in my gifts and callings in Christ Jesus and to develop by your side as an effective colaborer in ministry. Thank you for patiently encouraging me to finish this book and for all the hours you have spent listening to my dreams. Life with you has truly been a dream come true.

Crystal, Tiffany and Jason, I am so proud of each one of you! Thank you so much for all the times you have had to share my attention not only with this book but also with all that God has called me to do. It has been a joy of my heart to see you grow in the Lord and to see the special gifts He has placed in each of you begin to blossom. I love you bunches!

I would also like to express my love and appreciation for my mom and dad, Frank and Leona Makosky. Thanks for teaching me to be persistent in the face of difficulty and for imparting to me a sense of confidence that has helped me believe I can succeed as I follow my dreams. I love you both dearly.

Special thanks go to the staff and elders at Christian International Family Church for being a constant source of encouragement to me, both personally and in ministry, and for helping me find the time to finish this book.

Finally, I want to express my deep, heartfelt love and appreciation to my spiritual parents and mentors, Dr. Bill and Evelyn Hamon. Your vision, insight, wisdom, love and encouragement have meant the world to me. Thank you for inspiring me to be all that I am called to be and for continuously helping me press toward that mark. Thank you for the example that you have set for me and so many others and for every trail you have blazed that makes my path easier to walk.

CONTENTS

Chapter 15
Responding to Your Dreams and Visions
What does God want me to do with my dreams?
How can I really know God's will?
When should I share a dream about someone else?

Chapter 16
A Charge to Dreamers

Recommended Reading on
Dreams, Visions and Prophecy

FOREWORD

"Do you think God speaks to people today?"

This was the first question—almost the first words—spoken to me by a national political leader I met with recently. I was a bit taken aback. "Well, yes, I do," I replied. He wanted to know why I believed this, how one could be sure and the answers to a few other well-thought-out questions. It seems he had recently experienced some very detailed and interesting dreams about our nation. It was an enlightening meeting.

This leader's questions are not unusual. The proliferation of interest today in psychic reading, horoscopes, Eastern religions and various other attempts to contact the realm of the supernatural all attest to people's innate desire to hear from God. Many don't realize this is what (or Whom) they are seeking; but those of us who have had this need met by Him realize it is the Lord we all seek.

God does indeed speak to people today. The prophet Joel prophesied:

> And it shall come to pass in the last days, saith God, I will pour out of my Spirit upon all flesh: and your sons and your daughters shall prophesy, and your young men shall see visions, and your old men shall dream dreams: And on my servants and on my handmaidens I will pour out in those days of my Spirit; and they shall prophesy (Acts 2:17,18, *KJV*).

As the Holy Spirit is poured out in great measure on today's Church, we should anticipate God's speaking to us through prophetic dreams and visions. God is ready, by His Spirit, to expose the counterfeit and satisfy the yearnings of the human race to hear from Him. Once again the hunger and curiosity of the world represent opportunities for God and the Church.

The question is, Will we, the people of God, be ready with the answers they need? Or, as is sadly the case at times, must they resort to the counterfeit measures of Satan to satisfy their hunger? I pray that we will be prepared. If we are, it will be solid, balanced, biblical works such as this book that will help prepare us.

In the Scriptures, God often spoke through dreams and visions.

Jacob's life was radically impacted by a series of dreams.

God revealed Joseph's destiny through dreams.

Another Joseph, Christ's stepfather, was instructed through dreams at least four times concerning issues surrounding the birth of our Lord.

Unrighteous King Nebuchadnezzar dreamed dreams from the Almighty.

Pilate's wife—probably not a follower of Jehovah—was warned in a dream about her husband's dealings with Christ.

The apostles Peter, Paul and John were given visions by the Holy Spirit.

The Scriptures contain more than 50 references to God's sending messages to people through dreams or visions! He assures us that in the last days this will continue.

Yes, we can expect God to speak to us today through dreams and visions. Obvious and appropriate questions then arise:

- How do we know when a dream or vision is from God?
- How do we recognize false messages in dreams?

- How do we interpret our dreams?
- What do we do when a dream contains a warning?
- How do we steward such subjective ways of hearing from God?

These questions deserve answers. In fact, not knowing the answers has probably scared off sincere Christians, including leaders, more than anything else, from seriously considering the meaning of their dreams.

As a pastor I have found the prophetic to be a very challenging aspect of the Spirit's work to steward. The subjectivity of the prophetic lends itself to abuses, and I've had my share of questionable "words from the Lord" given to me by well-meaning people. The temptation—I've seen it done and have done it myself—is to shy away from the prophetic to avoid such mistakes and abuses. Nothing could make Satan happier!

Our inability and/or unwillingness to hear from the Lord today is the primary cause of an anemic Church. Proverbs 29:18 (*KJV*) tells us, "Where there is no vision, the people perish." The word "vision" in this verse is translated from the Hebrew word *chazown* and means much more than just a vision or plan for the future. It is literally any communication from the Lord, regardless of the means of delivery, including dreams, visions and any other form of revelation. Where communication from the Lord is not present, destruction, ruination and death result. Perish the thought! Satan knows this and uses every available means to stop us from receiving God's words, including fostering fears of abuses and inaccuracy.

This is why I appreciate my friend Jane Hamon's book *Dreams and Visions* so much. She has given us a masterful work to use in stewarding these important aspects of hearing from the Holy Spirit. In fact, I think it is so well done that I am prepared to make an unusual statement: In my 25 years of study and training, I have found no book or teaching aid on this subject that is as biblical, thorough, practical and scholarly as *Dreams and Visions*.

Who should read this book?

1. Every Christian who wants to understand his or her dreams—and how God may use them to speak to us today.
2. Pastors, teachers, church leaders and Christian counselors—all who have a calling to train, equip and instruct the Body of Christ in the ways of the Lord. Pastor, you especially need no longer fear stewarding these important but subjective ways by which the Spirit speaks.

Thank you, Jane, for this extremely important and valuable labor of love. I endorse this superb book with joy, knowing that many will greatly benefit from it. Thank you!

DUTCH SHEETS
Colorado Springs, Colorado

INTRODUCTION

In 1980, while at college in Dallas, Texas, I dreamed a very disturbing dream. In my dream I saw my younger brother become very ill and die. I woke up with tears flowing down my face, and I began to pray for him. The next day my mother called from home in another state to say that the night before, my brother's appendix had ruptured while he was on a camping trip. By the time they rushed him to the hospital he had become extremely ill and could very well have died! It suddenly occurred to me that God had spoken to me through my dream!

Dreams and visions have long fascinated people because of their mysterious nature. Kings have inquired of them, philosophers have theorized about them, prophets have expounded from them, and scientists have studied them.

The Scriptures show us that God often used dreams and visions to communicate His divine messages to man. On numerous occasions these secret, hidden mysteries contained revelations that impacted the very course of history!

I have long been intrigued by dreams, especially as I often dreamed in great detail and with intricate and exciting plots. In 1980, however, I began to have dreams which would then come to pass in my waking life shortly thereafter. I was also seeing things in dreams of which I had no natural knowledge, which I would later find to be true. It was then I embarked on a journey of understanding how God was personally speaking to me concerning my life and the lives of others through dreams and visions.

God desires to communicate with us through dreams and visions, but it is only as we gain understanding of how to unlock the secret, hidden mysteries that we will be able to take full advantage of what He is saying.

Recently, the Body of Christ has become more and more aware that we are experiencing revelation given through dreams and visions. Acts 2:17,18 declares:

> And it shall come to pass in the last days, says God, that I will pour out of My Spirit on all flesh; your sons and your daughters shall prophesy, your young men shall see visions, your old men shall dream dreams. And on My menservants and on My maidservants I will pour out My Spirit in those days; and they shall prophesy.

The outpouring of the Holy Spirit and the subsequent manifestations of prophecy, dreams and visions are actually the fulfillment of biblical promises! Jesus promised His followers that He would send a comforter, a *paraklete*, one who would walk beside them. On the day of His ascension into heaven He told His disciples to go wait for the promise of the Father. Dreams, visions and prophecy are part of that wonderful promise!

We are now living in a day in which God is pouring out His Spirit upon men and women of all nations in new measure. We have seen a greater release of God's prophetic voice, both through His prophets and His prophetically gifted people, than has ever been seen before. With this fresh anointing has come an increase of other manifestations of the Holy Spirit, such as the dreaming of dreams and the seeing of visions.

During the last several decades modern psychologists have studied dreams and discovered many interesting secrets regarding the workings of the subconscious mind. Though their research has produced much understanding of the technical evaluation of dreams, this book is not written from a psychological perspective but, rather, will investigate how God speaks to us through our dreams.

I have personally experienced many dreams and visions, and during the last several years I have gained a greater understanding of how to interpret these revelations through a careful study of the Scriptures, through reading Christian materials on the subject and through recording many of my own dreams. I do not esteem myself to be an expert in dream interpretation, though I have interpreted dreams for many people. However, I do believe that individuals should examine their own dreams and learn to listen to God's Holy Spirit through this God-ordained method of communication.

This book will not attempt to answer every detail and technical question regarding dreams and visions, for each individual's dreams are extremely different and the symbolism therein may vary greatly. However, I hope to show that Bible-believing Christians need to begin to listen to the language of their dreams and to be aware that God may be communicating to them through visions.

If we are indeed in the last days, we must begin to recognize God's purpose and intention for dreams and visions, how to relate to them and how to properly respond to what has been revealed. As we begin to learn to discern the voice of God in dreams and visions, we will reap the benefits of a closer, more intimate walk with our Lord (see Hebrews 5:14).

And ye shall seek me, and find me, when ye shall search for me with all your heart (Jeremiah 29:13, *KJV*).

This book is primarily directed to those who are in relationship with God through our Lord and Savior, Jesus Christ.

Therefore, if you have not yet made a commitment of your life to Jesus Christ, I want to invite you to pray the following prayer and receive His gift of eternal life:

Heavenly Father, I thank You for Your great love that You have for me. I recognize that I am a sinner and that I need You to come into my life and make me new. Forgive me for living my life according to my own way instead of how You desire me to live. I repent of my sin and I receive the gift of eternal life which You have made available through Jesus Christ. I believe Jesus came to earth, lived a sinless life, was crucified and shed His blood for my sins and that He rose again, triumphing over death, hell and the grave. Thank You for making me a part of Your family. I now receive You into my life as my personal Savior, Lord and King and I receive Your Holy Spirit who will lead me and guide me into all truth. In Jesus' name. Amen!

GOD'S PURPOSE FOR DREAMS AND VISIONS

If there is a prophet among you, I, the LORD, make Myself known to him in a vision; I speak to him in a dream.

NUMBERS 12:6

God has always desired to communicate with His people. Yet for centuries God was thought of as a silent, distant, almost indifferent Creator who ruled the affairs of the universe and, though omnipotent, took little interest in the day-to-day lives of His children.

At the dawn of a new millennium, the Church has become increasingly aware that God not only *wants* to speak to His people but also that He is, in fact, concerned with even the smallest details of our lives:

> Are not five sparrows sold for two copper coins? And not one of them is forgotten before God. But the very hairs of your head are all numbered. Do not fear therefore; you are of more value than many sparrows (Luke 12:6,7).

From the beginning and throughout Scripture we see a God who cares and who communicates His concerns, His direction, His judgments and His blessings to the people of this world. At times He spoke directly to His servants; other times His mouth-pieces, the prophets, delivered His messages. Judges, kings, priests and even musicians carried God's instructions to the people. And in numerous instances in Scripture, God directed, corrected and instructed individuals through dreams and visions.

Dreams and visions are perhaps the most common ways God has communicated with man. The Bible contains more than 50 references to dreams and visions in which God delivered messages. Abraham learned of his promised lineage through dreams and visions. Jacob's life was drastically changed through a series of dreams in which he received God's promises regarding his heritage. God revealed Joseph's destiny through his dreams. Daniel, Obadiah, Nahum and Zechariah were among the prophets often visited with revelations from God through visions and dreams.

Great protection was given the Christ child as God's messengers spoke to Joseph and the Magi in dreams. The apostles Peter, Paul and John were later visited by the Spirit of God in visions.

What Are Dreams?

Webster's Dictionary defines a dream as "a succession of images or ideas present in the mind during sleep." Dreams are formed in the subconscious mind of a man or woman based on images and symbols which are unique to the individual, depending on his or her background, experience and current life circumstances.

Dreams can communicate to us truth about ourselves—or others—which our conscious mind may have failed to acknowledge. One word for dreams in the Greek language was *enupnion*, which was defined as "something seen in sleep or a vision in a dream."

Dreams can originate strictly within the natural mind or can be given as messages from God's Spirit and received within the mind of man. They are not always easy to understand, but dreams are one means by which God may choose to speak to us.

What Are Visions?

Webster's Dictionary defines a vision as "the act or power of perceiving abstract or invisible subjects as clearly as if they were visible objects." A vision is also defined as "foresight." One Hebrew word for vision is *chizzayown*, which literally means "a revelation." A Greek word translated as "vision" in the New Testament, *horasis*, means "the act of gazing at something or an inspired appearance."

Dreams and visions are basically the same except that a dream occurs during periods of sleep, while a vision generally refers to images or revelations received in picture form while a person is awake.

I have often heard people say that they had a dream just before getting out of bed in the morning, only they weren't sure whether it was a dream since they thought they were awake at the time. Whether these were dreams or visions is immaterial. More important is the message of the revelation.

Joshua 1:8 tells us to meditate upon God's Word both day and night. Often, nocturnal meditation will result in receiving revelation through a dream. At times this may be a divine revelation—i.e., God speaking to you through the dream. Or it may be a personal revelation—your subconscious mind revealing your deepest, innermost thoughts. Psalm 16:7 confirms this, saying:

I will bless the LORD who has given me counsel; my heart [thoughts or inner man] also instructs [counsels] me in the night seasons.

Communication of Dreams

Dreams are messages sent either from God's Spirit or from your own soul, which comprises your mind, will and emotions. The subconscious mind within your soul provides the background or screen for these messages to be broadcast on.

Spiritual dreams are inspired by God, then communicated to our subconscious minds. These must then be received and discerned by our conscious minds through the inspiration of the Holy Spirit. Just as television and radio waves which are broadcast through the air must be tuned in to be received and enjoyed, dreams are constantly being broadcast to our subconscious minds, both by God's Spirit and by our own souls. We must learn to turn on our receivers and tune in the messages being sent.

The prophet Micah said that he "saw" the word of the Lord (Micah 1:1). How did he see this word? The *New International Version* calls this a vision. Micah likely saw images or pictures projected on the screen of his mind, which communicated God's word to him.

If we compare the communication of the Spirit of the Lord through dreams to other methods of divine communication mentioned in Scripture—prophecy, a word of knowledge, etc.— the primary difference is that dreams are given first to our subconscious minds before being perceived by our conscious minds.

Remembering Our Dreams

Many people tell me they do not hear from God in dreams because they don't generally remember their dreams. And when they *do* remember a dream, they recall only fragmented portions—scattered images or happenings which don't make much sense in the light of day. This is seen in Scripture when Nebuchadnezzar, king of Babylon, had a dream that disturbed him a great deal, yet he couldn't recall what he had dreamed. But God showed the dream to Daniel and gave him the interpretation as well (see Daniel 2:1-47).

Job 20:8 describes the fleeting nature of dreams:

> He will fly away like a dream, and not be found; yes, he
> will be chased away like a vision of the night.

Sleep specialists tell us that everyone dreams for a period of time while in REM (rapid eye movement) sleep. So if all of us dream every night at some point, why don't we recall what has been dreamed? There are several explanations. One explanation is that God created the mind to be constantly active, 24 hours a day, making it unlikely that every thought or image that flashes across the mind, whether conscious or subconscious, is meant to be remembered and studied.

Another explanation could be that because dreams have not been taken seriously by much of our culture, as products of this culture we allow our conscious minds to reject dreams as unimportant and quickly forget them. In effect, we turn off our receivers.

Often, a person does not immediately understand a dream, so he or she assumes it has no significance and dismisses it from the conscious mind, neglecting to search for any meaning therein. As you read this book, it is important that you begin to understand that dreams are often conveyed in our subconscious minds in a symbolic fashion and that it will take time to develop a workable understanding of your own personal language of symbols.

Yet another reason we may not always remember our dreams could be because we do not choose to remember them in a timely manner. Scientists have established that chemicals called serotonin and norepinephrine exist in the memory banks of the brain for the purpose of transferring a thought from short-term memory to long-term memory. If a thought, or in this case, a dream, is reinforced or purposely remembered through rehearsal, these chemicals "print" that dream in the long-term memory bank. If this does not occur immediately after waking, then there is a good possibility that the dream will be lost and forgotten. If a dream is stored in your long-term memory, you will find it easier to call to mind later.

Sometimes, however, this memory method may fail. I have on several occasions awakened in the night with a dream I desired to remember. As I lay in bed and went over the dream in my mind, I have felt confident that it would be impossible to forget a dream of such insight and clarity. Nevertheless, when I awoke in the morning I could not recall even the most general details of the dream.

If you are serious about understanding your dreams, you should be prepared for such instances by keeping a notebook and pencil by the bed. Then, when you awaken in the middle of the night, you can record the dream and safely go back to sleep, knowing the dream and its details will be waiting for you to explore in the morning.

Of course, we may have difficulty remembering our dreams, even after we have recognized God as the source, simply because we lack the desire to hear His voice. We must not be apathetic or dull of hearing when our heavenly Father is speaking to us. We must allow God to give us that hunger that can only be quenched by communing with Him. Hearing and responding to the voice of the Lord never fails to intensify the intimacy of a relationship with Him.

God Is Still Speaking Today!

God is still speaking today and uses a variety of means to communicate with us. He speaks from both the Logos (the written Word) and the *rhema* word of God (a timely, Holy Spirit-inspired word, often from the written Word or via the gifts of the Spirit). He will speak through an inner witness in our spirit. He will speak to us through godly counsel and through biblical preaching. God will also use nature, circumstances and godly authority to speak into our lives, but we must have ears to hear and hearts to receive what He is saying.

> We may have difficulty remembering our dreams simply because we lack the desire to hear God's voice.

The Bible accounts show many reasons why God sends messages through dreams and visions.

Primarily, of course, it's because He has something to communicate to us. He may be teaching us regarding personal areas of our lives, exposing external mannerisms that may need to change, revealing areas where we are to concentrate our prayers and intercession, or teaching us more about His love and His plan for our lives. The messages He desires to convey to us are often unique and varied.

God will use our dreams to bring instruction and counsel to us, even as we sleep. In Scripture, God Himself often appeared to individuals in dreams. On other occasions the angel of the Lord appeared to individuals in dreams (see Genesis 28:10-16; 2 Chronicles 1:7).

God also spoke through symbolic dreams to such worldly men as Nebuchadnezzar, as well as to godly men like Joseph (he of the "technicolor dreamcoat") and Daniel. These men had divine encounters with their Creator through dreams that required an interpretation in order for them to benefit from the message contained therein.

An ordinary Nazarene carpenter with no formal religious training, Joseph dreamed dreams regarding Mary and the baby Jesus in which an angel gave specific instruction concerning the child's well-being and safety (see Matthew 1,2).

God still speaks today through dreams and visions, but only those who have their hearts and spirits tuned to His Spirit will hear and receive all that God has for them.

Chapter 2

DREAMS, VISIONS AND PROPHECY

I have also spoken by the prophets, and have multiplied visions; I have given symbols through the witness of the prophets.

HOSEA 12:10

David Yonggi Cho, pastor of the world's largest church in Seoul, South Korea, has said, "Pictures are the language of the Holy Spirit." The word "vision" in Hosea 12:10 comes from the Hebrew word *chazown*, which means "revelation, an oracle, a dream or vision"—all ways in which God uses pictures to speak to His people.

Right now, you may be saying to yourself, *Pictures I understand. I mean, everybody dreams. But who am I to hear from God? Don't you have to be somebody special, like a prophet? Are there real prophets anymore? What is a prophecy anyway?* All excellent questions. Let's start with the last one first.

Prophecy in its simplest terms is defined as "God communicating His thoughts and intents to mankind," or as "God speaking."[1] As we have seen, God often chose individuals to hold the ministry office of prophet—Samuel, Daniel, Deborah, Nehemiah, John the Baptist, to name a few—to stand as God's representatives and deliver God's spoken word to individuals, groups and even cities and nations. But He also chose to speak directly to very ordinary men and women to communicate His purposes.

The term "prophetic dream" is used to refer to a dream through which God has spoken to an individual in order to communicate a divine message. This message may have to do with the dreamer and his or her life, or about another person or situation. The Bible tells us the purpose for prophecy is to bring edification, exhortation and comfort to the followers of Christ (see 1 Corinthians 14:3). Therefore, a dream that encourages, exhorts or comforts and is biblical in context may be considered a prophetic dream.

Yet many people have difficulty accepting the idea that dreams hold any significance for their lives. One reason for this is that they don't often remember their dreams. Another is they don't understand the parts they *do* remember. As a result, dreams are typically rejected as nonsense.

As a matter of fact, most of us have used the phrase "Don't worry, it's just a dream" at one time or another, dismissing our own dreams or the dreams of others as merely figments of the imagination—fantasies conjured up by the subconscious mind that are best ignored.

From childhood, we have been erroneously taught that dreams don't really mean anything, that they are unimportant and have little or no relevance to our lives. This is not necessarily the fault of our parents but more an indication of the philosophic and scientific thought of our Western culture, which has been slow to develop an understanding of the language of symbolism that is vital to dream interpretation.

A History of Prophetic Dreams and Visions

About 400 B.C., the Greek philosopher Plato set forth the premise that there are three ways to obtain valid knowledge: by way of the five senses, through reasoning of the mind and from the spirit realm. Fifty years later Aristotle came along and revised this notion. He believed that the five senses and reason were actually the only valid means of obtaining true knowledge, completely ruling out any credence to the idea that we may gain knowledge through spiritual means.

This teaching was carried down through the centuries until it became rooted in European thought and culture and eventually crept its way into the Church, banishing any doctrines which taught the spontaneous flow of revelation through the Spirit of God, including prophecy, healing, and tongues and interpretation. Visions and dreams were relegated to the territory of the flesh—at best mere products of the imagination.

Miracles and prophecies still happened here and there in Europe and, later, in America, particularly at times of revival or awakenings. But it wasn't until God began pouring out His Spirit in the early 1900s that the Church at large began to reawaken to the realities of the gifts of the Holy Spirit. Ordinary men and women of God once again spoke with new tongues, received words of revelation knowledge, dreamed prophetic dreams and saw visions. God released His supernatural power in healing and miracles through such men as Oral Roberts and T. L. Osborne. With the rise of the charismatic movement, the gift of prophecy began to be recognized both in presbytery and congregational settings.

In recent years, a number of gifted individuals have been recognized as appointed by God to the office of prophet and have operated effectively in this ministry. This prophetic movement, which continues to grow, has helped reestablish the biblical truths regarding God's desire and willingness to speak to mankind in a personal way. In addition to raising up new prophets, God is releasing among His people the ability to hear

Hearing the voice of
God is vital to the
Christian walk of a
growing number of
believers.

His voice more clearly and receive prophetic insight through the Holy Spirit.

After many centuries of darkness, the Church has once again begun to look to the spiritual realm as a valid source of knowledge. Where once the occult was the dominant, albeit illegitimate, source of "revelations" of the future, the Church is now rising to receive godly, prophetic insight into spiritual and natural matters through the gifts of the Holy Spirit. Along with this outpouring of God's Spirit has come a desire within His people to understand what He may be saying to them in their dreams. Hearing the voice of God for ourselves—and for others—has become a vital part of the Christian walk for a growing number of believers.

Unfortunately, many in the Church still believe God to be a silent observer of human affairs; thus they have resolutely closed themselves off from receiving any gift from God's Spirit. Sadly enough, many of these same Christians dabble in occultic methods for obtaining revelation: horoscopes, tarot card readings, Ouija boards, palm readings and the like. They claim to indulge in these practices "just for fun" yet never fail to share in astonishment any seemingly accurate information they receive.

Dreams Are Evidence of the Holy Spirit in Operation

This is what was spoken by the prophet Joel: "And it shall come to pass in the last days, says God, that I will pour out of My Spirit on all flesh; your sons and your daughters shall prophesy, your young men shall see visions, your old men shall dream dreams" (Acts 2:16,17).

The apostle Peter spoke these words on the Day of Pentecost after the Holy Spirit was poured out on 120 disciples of Christ who had gathered together in Jerusalem. Peter identified this outpouring of the Spirit to be the fulfillment of a prophecy given in Joel 2:28 and proclaimed that the gift of the Holy Spirit was for *all* who would believe in Christ, without respect of persons (see Acts 2:38,39). Prophecies, dreams and visions would be given to male and female, young and old alike.

As the Church today becomes more and more conscious of the workings of the Holy Spirit, many are only beginning to realize that God is speaking to them during their sleep. We cannot discount the validity of dreams as a means of receiving spiritual insight, for the Bible tells us God's people "are destroyed for lack of knowledge" (Hosea 4:6).

Think of the consequences if Joseph had ignored the dream in which he was told to take Mary and the baby Jesus to Egypt to protect the child's life (see Matthew 2:13). What if King Abimelech had discarded the dream concerning Sarah, Abraham's wife (see Genesis 20)? The lineage from which the Messiah was to come could have been corrupted. God's plans would have been greatly affected had these men not taken seriously the warnings spoken to them in their sleep.

Dreams Are Not an Indication of Spirituality

Not only do you not have to be someone special to hear from God, but it is also important to note that a propensity for dreaming is not an indication of one's spirituality or right standing with God. Science tells us that nearly everyone dreams approximately one hour per night. Some dream more; some less. Some have a greater capacity to remember what they've dreamed; some have less. Nevertheless, everyone dreams each night with few exceptions. Dreams, like rain, fall on the godly and the sinner, the righteous and the unrighteous.

God spoke to the wife of Pontius Pilate in a dream, warning her husband not to have anything to do with Jesus (see Matthew 27:19). We have no way of knowing her spiritual condition, although it seems unlikely she was a follower of Christ.

King Abimelech and his house were under the curse of God. Because Abraham feared for his life, he had deceived the Philistine king, claiming that Sarah, his wife, was in fact his sister. Abimelech was taken with Sarah and intended to make her his wife. However, before he consummated the marriage, God spoke to this king of Gerar:

> But God came to Abimelech in a dream by night, and said to him, "Indeed you are a dead man because of the

woman whom you have taken, for she is a man's wife"
(Genesis 20:3).

King Abimelech heeded the dream and repented of his mistake by returning Sarah to her husband. A dream from God
commanded the attention and obedience of this mighty, wealthy
king. He tried to make amends by sending Abraham and Sarah
on their way with a gift of sheep, oxen and servants and a thousand pieces of silver.

Abimelech was not necessarily a godly man (see v. 11), but he
recognized God's voice in his dream and took swift action to
make things right. The dream instilled the fear of God in him,
and because he cooperated with the Lord, he was blessed with
children and prospered (see vv. 17,18). Archeological finds have
shown that the land of Gerar was extremely prosperous during
the period of the patriarchs.

Thus, Scripture shows us that while dreams occur in all of
mankind, God can and will use dreams to speak to the unrighteous as well as the godly.

Do We Have Ears to Hear?

God delights in communicating with His people; therefore, we
must seek to increase our ability to listen to what He is saying. We
must realize that though we may not always have instant understanding of our dreams, we will be opening a great avenue of insight
into God's purposes for our lives if we would only take the time to
discern His methods for communicating through our dreams.

God is always speaking, but do we hear what He is saying?

Note
1. Bill Hamon, *Prophets and Personal Prophecy* (Shippensburg, PA: Destiny
   Image, 1987), p. 29.

Chapter 3

SPIRITUAL DREAMS AND VISIONS

There are those who believe that all dreams and visions are inspired by God. Others believe that dreams are strictly soulish in their origination, produced out of the subconscious mind, and that visions are nothing more than daydreams or products of an overactive imagination. Which of these, if either, is correct?

Scripture supports the idea that there are three different types of dreams and visions, each of which can be traced to different sources:

1. Spiritual dreams and visions, which are inspired by God's Spirit
2. Natural, or soulful, dreams and visions, which are produced by the natural processes of a person's mind, will and emotions
3. False or occultic dreams and visions, which are demon inspired or deceitfully crafted by evil men

As you learn to interpret your dreams, you will find it helpful to understand these different sources of inspiration to ensure a proper and balanced response.

A spiritual dream or vision is one that is motivated and inspired by God's Spirit and communicated through the natural mind to relay a divine message. This message can be a personal revelation, insight into a natural situation, or a foretelling of future events.

Pray That You May Interpret

Many who do not know how to interpret their dreams often have a difficult time grasping the concept of revelation coming through a series of seemingly meaningless and disjointed pictures, scenes and conversations. How can something which makes no sense to the natural mind contain revelation?

In this sense, I liken dreams to the gifts of tongues and interpretation of tongues, which are widely recognized as valid gifts of the Holy Spirit in operation in many churches today. The apostle Paul tells us in 1 Corinthians 14 that when Christians are gathered together and a message is given in an unknown tongue, the message will not bear fruit unless it is followed by an interpretation. The person speaking by God's Spirit is speaking mysteries which cannot bring edification, exhortation or comfort to the body unless interpreted. The tongue alone gives an uncertain message and though God may be speaking, the church body cannot benefit unless it can understand the meaning behind the message. Therefore, the tongue becomes of no effect or value unless an individual is yielded to the Holy Spirit to give an interpretation.

"Therefore," Paul writes, "let him who speaks in a tongue pray that he may interpret" (1 Corinthians 14:13).

Similarly, a dream can be a prophetic message to an individual, yet without a Spirit-led interpretation and proper application, the dream becomes of no effect or value.

Nebuchadnezzar's dreams would have been worthless, more of a burden than a blessing, had Daniel not been there to give the proper interpretation and application. Likewise, Pharaoh required someone with prophetic insight to interpret his dreams. Joseph enabled an entire region of the world to survive seven years of famine by discerning God's plan given through Pharaoh's dream.

Just as there are those who are gifted in tongues and interpretation, there are those who have been gifted with the ability to interpret dreams. Though we all may learn to interpret our dreams, God gives special enablements to some for this purpose. Joseph and Daniel were men anointed by God to interpret dreams that changed the destinies of nations. Without the utilization of their prophetic gifts, the dreams of their kings would have been received uncertainly and history may well have been affected.

Therefore, just as we are to pray that we may interpret tongues, so we should also pray to interpret our dreams. Though upon waking dreams may resonate with an uncertain sound or unclear meaning, once illumination is sought and given, the dreamer may receive edification from the dream.

Different Types of Spiritual Dreams

There are several types of spiritual dreams through which communication between God and man takes place. We will look at dreams which involve (1) God speaking to your spirit, (2) your spirit speaking to God, and (3) God interceding through your spirit.

1. God Speaking to Our Spirits

These are dreams which are prophetic in nature, originating with and birthed by God, which contain revelation for the dreamer about his life or circumstances, revelation for other individuals or even revelation for a corporate body of people. Similar to the purpose for prophecy, these dreams also have the purpose of edification, exhortation and comfort.

An example of a dream of this nature was given to me by a woman in a leadership position. She dreamed in great detail of our church body participating in a worship service. In her dream, we were having difficulty breaking through into God's presence; but as our new worship leader led us forward, we soon experienced the presence of God in such a way as we had never done before. The majesty of God was displayed in His train of glorious colors. This brought us into a new communion with one another as well as with our Lord.

This was a dream that encouraged the dreamer with the beauty of the presence of the Lord during this time of breakthrough in worship. It also blessed our worship leader and gave him confidence in his new position. Most importantly, however, this dream spoke of a new level of intensity of worship and a deeper manifestation of God's presence in the midst of our church that God desired to bring us into as we persevered in our praise.

The dream edified the dreamer, but also the dream and its message were prophetic to the entire church body. Interestingly, for several months following this dream, a number of prophetic leaders around the country spoke to us of a new level of worship and a new glory to be revealed in our midst, thus confirming the message of the dream.

"Hitler-Town" Dream

I had a spiritual dream in which a Hitler-type dictator came into our town and began to take over, one house at a time. He used different tactics at each house to cause the individuals to comply with his rule and deny the Lord. With some he used torture; with others he put them under siege, slowly wearing them down. Then he was at my door. I asked myself, *What will it take to get me to submit to him? What is my price?* He sent his troops in, but they didn't touch me. Instead they took my children away, knowing that this would be the most effective way to get to me. The dream ended with a voice asking, "What is your price to deny the Lord?"

This dream examines a fear shared by most mothers; however, it was speaking to me in some very specific areas of my life. One area involved my commitment to God in ministry and my commitment to my family. As a copastor of our church, I often struggle with this balance between ministry and family. While my family is my priority, I recognize that I cannot deny God's mandate on my life for ministry. This dream came at a time when I was feeling reticent about some of the things God was directing me to do, because I was uncertain how this involvement would affect my family life. This dream stirred me to examine how I would respond to the Lord and His calling upon my life and how I would balance the responsibilities of my family.

Beyond this personal message, however, the Lord challenged me, showing that He was putting this same question to the Body of Christ: What is your price to deny the Lord and compromise your calling? Believers often say they would gladly die for their Lord, but when it comes to being obedient in some very simple areas, they cannot seem to make a commitment. This dream was a message not only to me personally but also to the corporate Body of Christ.

2. Our Spirits Crying Out to God

A second type of spiritual dream is when one's spirit or soul cries out to God in a dream. In a dream of this type, the redeemed spirit (or unredeemed spirit, in the case of an unbeliever) may be calling for needed assistance or may simply be expressing the inner thoughts of the soul. Such dreams usually originate in the spirit as a cry for God's intervention in our lives, whether through direction, correction or instruction.

A woman I once counseled had a recurring dream that she would wake up paralyzed—unable to move, speak or even pray. She would try to call on the Lord for help but was unable to even speak the name of Jesus. She was desperate for divine intervention in her life in these dreams. When I asked her if she felt helpless or paralyzed over situations in her life, she replied tearfully that she did. These dreams were her cries to God for help in situations she felt were out of her control.

Again, most of our dreams are personal dreams, which may bring self-revelation and instruction. These dreams may reveal to us hidden parts of our soulful nature or even parts of our spiritual nature that we may otherwise fail to recognize.

Shooting the Man of Faith

I once dreamed that I shot a man of God who is known for his tremendous teachings on faith. I then threw the gun away and tried to cover up my crime. I didn't know this man personally, but I knew what his teachings represented to me: my walk of faith.

God used this dream, which originated in my spirit, to reveal certain things to me about the condition of my own soul. It helped me to pinpoint areas where I had "assassinated" my own faith and then tried to cover it up. These specific areas were not found in the dream; however, the dream was a catalyst whereby God was able to reach me and bring clear revelation.

The dream helped me to understand situations I had been praying about without seeing any answers to my prayers. God heard my heart's cry and was able to stir my spirit to reveal keys to overcome my lack of faith and to receive His promises and provision to me.

3. God's Spirit Interceding Through Our Spirits

Sometimes God's Spirit will use dreams to alert us to needs for intercession. Romans 8:26 tells of the Spirit interceding through us with "groanings which cannot be uttered." When we pray, we may not have a clear understanding of why we feel a burden to allow the Spirit of God to pray through us, yet we feel an urgency to intercede on behalf of another. At times our dreams will wake us and alert us to begin to pray.

I have personally experienced dreams dealing with life and death

I awoke with tears streaming down my face, and I began to pray for my brother.

numerous times in my life. In one dream I saw my brother killed in a car accident where his car rolled and crushed him. I awoke with tears streaming down my face, and I began to pray for my brother. The next day, I received a cross-country call from my mother. She told me that my brother had been in a serious car accident earlier that day. His car had been struck and rolled over—but my brother stepped out without injury!

I believe prayer changes things. God alerted me through my dream and, at least in part, because of my obedience to pray and come into agreement with God's purposes for my brother, God spared his life.

We must be sensitive to the leading of the Spirit of God and obedient to pray when our spirits are stirred, for this is yet another way God will communicate His heart to us.

A woman once had a dream in which God caused her spirit to intercede for her sister in her dreams. She dreamed that her sister began to have a seizure and fell to the ground. In the dream, this woman laid hands on her sister and prayed for her, rebuking the sickness and imploring the Lord to heal her. It was quite a lengthy time of prayer in the dream, but as she finished praying, her sister became well.

The next day, her sister, who was in another state at the time, fell and began to have a seizure. In a short period of time, however, she came out of the seizure and was fine. In this case, intercession that went forth the night before in a dream perhaps prevented further difficulties or complications.

Many dreams are not so literal in their interpretation but are highly symbolic. Nevertheless, God can use your dreams to bring insight, illumination, revelation and edification to your spirit and soul as you attune your ear to God's Spirit.

Chapter 4

NATURAL DREAMS
AND VISIONS

Not all dreams contain revelation sent from God. When we are awake, not all of our thoughts are God's thoughts running through our minds. Likewise, when we sleep, the natural mind continues to process natural thoughts. Things that have happened in our past, people we have known, situations we are currently dealing with, circumstances or people that are upsetting us—all are things that may influence us to experience certain natural dreams.

Not all visions are from God either, but they may in fact be products of our natural minds or imaginations. Some people are very adept at daydreaming or escaping into a world of fantasy by allowing their minds to wander and create plots, places, conversations and experiences. These experiences can seem so real that the individual may not even be aware of what is happening around them.

These dreams and visions are not produced or influenced by the Spirit of God but by the soul, which contains the mind, will and emotions of an individual. Nevertheless, these can have great influence upon our natural minds. There are several ways our natural minds may influence us, particularly in the area of dreams.

Natural Dreams Reflect the Day's Activities

Ecclesiastes 5:3 tells us that a dream may come "through much activity" (or, as the *King James Version* puts it, "through the multitude of business"), when our minds are occupied with certain problems or circumstances. In such dreams, one may find a solution to a problem or even find lost objects. This does not necessarily indicate divine revelation but may be the subconscious mind dealing with the situation at hand or calling to remembrance the place where the missing object was last left. These are often referred to as soulish dreams.

Since dreams are related through our subconscious minds, it stands to reason that that which we have been thinking on will often be the subject of our dreams. During times of intense spiritual warfare, the content of my dreams will often have to do with situations involving the dark forces of the enemy. During times of heavy ministry, I often find myself praying and ministering all night long in my dreams. These are not necessarily spiritual dreams; they could merely be my mind rehearsing the day's activities.

As we sleep, our subconscious minds continue to work through and process the vast amounts of sensory, emotional and intellectual information we have gathered during the day. It is reported that the man who discovered organic chemistry struggled with incorrect formulas for a lengthy period of time and finally found his solution in a dream. Again, this may have been God speaking, but it is more likely that the man's subconscious mind continued to work on the solution to his dilemma long after his conscious mind was at rest.

There are other examples of soulish, carnal revelations received from dreams. Elias Howe got the idea for a machine that sews after he dreamed of being captured by savages who carried spears with holes in their tips. From this he derived the idea of putting a hole in the front end of a needle rather than at the back end or middle and invented the sewing machine.

Robert Louis Stevenson was inspired by a dream to write *The Strange Case of Dr. Jekyll and Mr. Hyde*. It is questionable whether this dream was inspired by God. Possibly, Stevenson's own soul may have been exposing a dark side of his personality through this dream. The result, in any case, was a classic piece of literature.

Sometimes dreams reflect that which has been said or done during the day. People we may have met or things we may have seen often appear in dreams without great spiritual significance as the mind, will and emotions continue to process such information.

In a dream I had as a child, I had fallen asleep in front of the TV and dreamed of a new invention that was like a handheld brush that blew air and could be used for styling your hair. When I woke up, I was excited because I had this great idea for a portable hair dryer and wanted to share it with someone. Fortunately, before I had an opportunity to tell anyone about my inspired invention, I saw a television commercial advertising the new blow-dryers which had just come out. Apparently, in my semiconscious state I had seen this commercial and then dreamed about inventing the blow-dryer.

This was merely my subconscious mind calling to remembrance something my conscious mind did not even remember seeing. While God may have been pointing out my creative abilities through this dream, I believe this dream was soulish in nature rather than spiritual.

Natural Dreams May Reflect Physical Needs

In saying that not every dream is a spiritual message from God, we should look at how our physical bodies can contribute to what is produced in our dream lives. You may have heard the term "pizza dreams," which usually refers to dreams inspired either by situations or by the food we have eaten before bedtime. Sleep specialists have noted that certain foods and some medications can affect dream patterns. These are natural dreams, motivated by natural stimuli or activities.

Not every dream is a spiritual message from God.

One woman I spoke with reported that anytime she took a certain over-the-counter medication she experienced horrible nightmares. When she stopped taking the medication, the bad dreams also stopped. A few months later, she tried taking the medicine again and had the same reaction, experiencing unsettling, even horrifying dreams. These dreams were clearly a result of a stimulant to her bodily system.

Isaiah 29:8 tells us:

> It shall even be as when a hungry man dreams, and look—he eats; but he awakes, and his soul is still empty; or as when a thirsty man dreams, and look—he drinks; but he awakes, and indeed he is faint.

Sometimes a bodily need, such as hunger or thirst, can prompt a dream. I once heard of someone who dreamed that she woke up and got out of bed to use the bathroom. The dream seemed so real that she had an accident. I do not feel that any spiritual significance should be assigned to such a dream. This was merely the subconscious mind responding to signals sent by the body and her physical body responding to her subconscious thoughts.

One night during a several-day fast, I dreamed of great tables of my favorite foods set before me. Some may say that this dream was addressing my spiritual hunger and the provision which God had made to fill that hunger. Perhaps; but the dream could also have been a natural response from my subconscious mind, letting me know that my body was hungry.

In another dream I was outside during the winter and had not dressed warmly enough. I remember running toward my house to get out of the cold. I would huddle next to trees and big rocks looking for any small measure of warmth. When I awoke, shivering, I discovered that my husband had once again pulled the covers off my side of the bed. Some may try to attach some spiritual significance to the dream, but it is much more likely that my subconscious was responding to the fact that I was cold!

Dreams Reflect the Heart's Meditation

Often, we may become so busy dealing with the activities of daily living that we don't take time to slow down and deal with ongoing issues that may be bothering us. As we sleep, our subconscious minds will often seize the opportunity and cause us to consider our perspectives on bothersome problems.

Hurtful or traumatic experiences from the past may show up in our dreams. At times God will use these natural dreams to bring a spiritual message to you. Other times our dreams may act as reminders that we still have areas of hurt or wounding that must be tended to if we are to be emotionally healthy.

Since that which we have allowed our minds to mull over and dwell upon during the day will often later appear in our dreams, it is important for us to spend our waking hours meditating upon the right things. If you are not receiving any spiritual insight in your sleep and rarely experience dreams having to do with spiritual matters, you may want to investigate what you are allowing your mind to meditate on. God has commanded that we should meditate upon His Word day and night:

> This Book of the Law shall not depart from your mouth, but you shall meditate in it day and night, that you may observe to do according to all that is written in it. For then you will make your way prosperous, and then you will have good success (Joshua 1:8).

As we partake of and digest the Word of God during the day, our minds will continue during the night to assimilate the truths we have read. Psalm 119:55 says, "I remember Your name in the night, O LORD." Read and meditate on the Bible, and your dreams will take God's truths and apply them to areas of your natural life. And as you heed God's words to you, you will experience His life-changing power.

Chapter 5

FALSE DREAMS
AND VISIONS

"Behold, I am against those who prophesy false dreams," says the LORD, "and tell them, and cause My people to err by their lies."

JEREMIAH 23:32

For the idols speak delusion; the diviners envision lies, and tell false dreams; they comfort in vain.

ZECHARIAH 10:2

The Bible clearly speaks of dreams which are false or even occultic in nature. A false dream or vision is one that attempts to establish ungodly principles or deception concerning biblical truth in the mind of the dreamer or in those to whom the dreamer tells the dream.

In examining the word "false" in the above Scripture verses, we find two different types of false dreams. The word "false" in Jeremiah 23:32 is from a Hebrew word which indicates someone telling an untruth, a purposeful deceit or a lie—in short, a sham. These purported visions are given in order to manipulate or influence individuals toward an ungodly way of thinking for the deceiver's best interest. These are not visions at all but proceed from a wicked imagination or by twisting other real truths or valid visions to suit a selfish or demonic purpose.

The word "false" in Zechariah 10:2 indicates a destructive evil, idolatry or deception. Such dreams and visions may originate in the wicked, deceptive imaginations of a man's heart or could indicate a demonic manifestation speaking false and lying words.

The Word of God puts false dreamers and false prophets in the same category, telling us that their purpose is to draw people after other gods:

> If there arises among you a prophet or a dreamer of dreams, and he gives you a sign or a wonder, and the sign or the wonder comes to pass, of which he spoke to you, saying, "Let us go after other gods"—which you have not known—"and let us serve them," you shall not listen to the words of that prophet or that dreamer of dreams, for the LORD your God is testing you to know whether you love the LORD your God with all your heart and with all your soul (Deuteronomy 13:1-3).

Some of these dreams or visions may be occultic or demonic in origin and may even attempt to convey their own prophetic messages. Some may come from our own carnal minds attempting to lead us away from God's principles and precepts. If anyone tries to teach or preach a message which has been inspired from a dream or vision, it is important to assure that that which is preached aligns with the written Word of God before receiving the message.

> [False] prophets prophesy lies in My name. I have not sent them, commanded them, nor spoken to them; they prophesy to you a false vision, divination, a worthless thing, and the deceit of their heart (Jeremiah 14:14).

A Caution to Dreamers

In seeking to understand our dreams, we must be cautious not to become dependent on or directed by our dreams on a daily basis. This is dangerous ground and can open an individual to a spirit of error and deception. Again, this is where a soulish dream can come and lead men astray by speaking to their heart's fleshly desires. Sound teaching instructs Christians to be careful that all revelation—including prophecies, dreams and visions—should be measured by the principles found in the Word of God. Galatians 1:8 warns us:

> But even if we, or an angel from heaven, preach any other gospel to you than what we have preached to you, let him be accursed.

One must be cautious not to be deceived by angels of light, who are actually demonic beings masquerading as messengers from God. God's Word will be your guide as you learn to discern between the two.

A good example of this is found in the history of the Mormon religion, which is based on "visions" received from the "angel" Moroni to a man named Joseph Smith. Through the doctrines received in these visions, a new religion was established. Had Joseph Smith measured these visions against the principles found in God's Word, he would have found that his new revelations were not consistent with the truth found in Scripture. Instead, millions have since followed his teachings.

Likewise, many well-meaning Christians have been led astray in their personal lives by incorrectly interpreting revelation given to them through dreams, visions, prophecies or even by a still, small inner voice, which they believe to be God's voice but, rather, may be their own unhealed, deceitful hearts speaking to them. Scripture tells us, "He who trusts in his own heart is a fool" (Proverbs 28:26).

"For My thoughts are not your thoughts, nor are your ways My ways," says the LORD (Isaiah 55:8).

We should never depend solely upon any prophetic means to lead us in our daily walk, although at times God may indeed choose to speak a word of direction to us through these means. We are to be led by the Spirit of God through personal prayer and the study of His Word, not by continuous dream interpretation or even prophecy. Only by daily following Jesus Christ and sound doctrine from His Word will we receive true revelation and true interpretation of spiritual dreams and visions when they come.

Never depend solely upon your dreams to lead you in your daily walk.

Dreams of Diviners

In a day when psychics and the New Age movement seem to be thriving, we must be careful where we seek revelation and truth. God is the only source of valid revelation. The dreams of diviners are inspired by unsanctified human thoughts (humanism) or by dark angels, and the people of God are not to be led by them.

Pastor and author John Watson sums up the Christian's responsibility to be discerning concerning the dreams of others:

> It is very important to be Bible-based, submissive, servant Christians. The test of our character will reflect into our dreams and our walk with God. Distortions can be limited by our submission to God and his people. The dreams of the rebellious are often dangerous.[1]

Nightmares

> The distinguishing trait of a nightmare is that the dreamer is in danger. Parents are the exception when they dream their babies are in trouble.[2]

God will occasionally use a dream that startles or frightens to get our attention. In some cases, God may have been trying to deal with the dreamer concerning a certain issue in his or her life for some period of time before the dream; but because of dullness of hearing or perhaps negligence to heed the voice of the Lord, the dreamer simply has not paid attention. Therefore, he or she has the unpleasant experience of what many call a nightmare, or bad dream.

As mentioned earlier, King Abimelech had a nightmare in which God told him he was "a dead man" for taking another man's wife (Genesis 20:3). The dream frightened him to the point that he not only returned Sarah to Abraham but also loaded them with riches by way of apology.

Not all nightmares are from God, however. Hidden areas of our subconscious mind, things we read or see or hear and areas of long-term or recent anxiety all can produce frightening dreams. Soulish nightmares, though fearful, can often hold a key that will unlock areas needing emotional release or healing and should therefore be examined, too.

Some nightmares, on the other hand, are avenues for tormenting demonic spirits to harass and rob a person of his or her inner peace and joy. I once struggled through a three-month period during which I had one terrifying dream after another. While I did discover areas of unseen fears in my life, these dreams went beyond the informational and actually caused such emotional conflict and confusion that I became afraid to sleep at night for fear of the dreams. I prayed and took spiritual authority over these dreams and enlisted others to pray with me until this spirit of harassment and torment was broken.

I don't believe these dreams were inspired by God, but God did cause me to confront hidden fears through this time of conflict. It is important to realize that not every startling dream is of evil origin but, rather, may be God dealing with unseen areas of our souls and causing us to face disturbing truths about ourselves. Why? "And you shall know the truth, and the truth shall make you free" (John 8:32).

Dealing with Nightmares

If you or someone you know is having difficulty dealing with harassing dreams which are producing fruits of fear, anxiety and terror, it is probable that these dreams are not from God but, rather, are either soulfully or demonically inspired. If you sense an area of your soul is being revealed, you should be careful to record these dreams and ask for God's guidance and direction concerning the interpretation and application of these dreams. If necessary, your pastor or counselor may be able to help you determine how best to deal with that which you discover.

Such nightmares may be a response to something you have allowed your mind to feed on—movies, books, television programs, ungodly thoughts, fears. These thoughts, once planted in your mind, can grow into fearful things and become areas where spirits of darkness can begin to torment and harass you. When dealing with thoughts brought on by a spirit of fear or other demonic spirits, Christians should know they have been given spiritual authority over such things by the Word of God:

> (For the weapons of our warfare are not carnal, but *mighty through God* to the pulling down of strong holds;) *casting down imaginations*, and every high thing that exalteth itself against the knowledge of God, and *bringing into captivity every thought* to the obedience of Christ (2 Corinthians 10:4,5, *KJV*, emphasis added).

> Therefore submit to God. Resist the devil and he will flee from you (James 4:7).

Diligent prayer and use of the sword of the Spirit—God's Word (see Ephesians 6:17)—will secure your release from torment. Seek prayerful support from others who can stand with you against such attacks. Believers of Christ do not need to suffer unnecessary torment from their own souls or at the hands of the enemy. Jesus provided for our healing and deliverance from all such harassment when He shed His blood on the cross and gave us power over all the works of darkness (see Luke 10:19). We must lay hold of the full provision He made for our spiritual liberty and walk in freedom from fear—even as we sleep!

Notes
1. John Watson, *Christian Dream Interpretation* (n.p., n.d.), p. 25.
2. "The Stuff That Dreams Are Made Of," *Newsweek* (August 14, 1989), p. 43.

Chapter 6

KNOWING THE SOURCE OF YOUR DREAMS

But solid food belongs to those who are of full age, that is, those who by reason of use have their senses exercised to discern both good and evil.

HEBREWS 5:14

There is no easy way to describe how to discern among dreams and visions those which are strictly soulish in nature, those which are demonic in origin and those that are Holy Spirit inspired. However, one can *learn* to discern among these through diligence and practice. Just as we are to exercise our spiritual gifts to learn to discern the voice of God, so with dreams and visions we can test them and even practice with them until we come to a place where it is possible to distinguish that which is from God and that which is from our own souls.

Determining Factors

Since dreams and visions can originate with different sources, how do you determine whether or not a particular dream or vision is prophetic or natural? Spiritual or soulful? Divinely or demonically inspired? Several indications found in God's Word will help to guide you in determining whether or not a revelation received is from God. The following are some questions which should be asked anytime you receive a dream, vision or revelation. These questions should also be asked when a "prophetic" message is communicated to you secondhand.

Is the message of the dream or vision consistent with doctrine, teachings and principles from the Word of God?

The written Word of God, the Bible, is the standard by which all revelation must be judged, for "all Scripture is given by inspiration of God, and is profitable for doctrine, for reproof, for correction, for instruction in righteousness" (2 Timothy 3:16).

We must realize that men and women all over the world hold many different opinions concerning how things should be, the nature of truth, and the moral and ethical standards we should live by. However, God's Word provides consistent guidelines that govern all mankind. When interpreting revelation it is important that the message in no way contradicts the precepts of God's Word.

All spiritual dreams or visions will support and emphasize biblical truth. If the dream you are interpreting does not, it is likely soulish in origin. Do not pore over the Bible, seeking some obscure passage which, taken out of context, confirms the dream; but examine the dream in the light of the whole Word of God.

Is the message of the dream or vision consistent with the teachings, character and nature of Jesus Christ?

A spiritual dream or vision will always magnify the person of Jesus Christ and His principles, which permeate the Word of God. Jesus came to liberate men and women from the letter of the Law. He came that mankind could be free so that all who receive Him might have peace. Any interpretation of a dream which would put individuals into bondage of any sort should be reevaluated based on Jesus' teachings and His undying love, which He showed for us and which He expects us to show for one another.

All revelation from spiritual dreams and visions will lead us into a closer, more committed relationship with our King. Any thought that comes from a vision or dream that makes Jesus less than the Son of God is erroneous, for He is our only way of salvation. Jesus said, "I am the way, the truth, and the life. No one comes to the Father except through Me" (John 14:6).

Does the message of the dream or vision lead one to righteousness?

From Genesis through Revelation, the Bible admonishes God's people to pursue righteousness, to lead a life which is free from sin (see 1 Timothy 6:11). This precludes both sins of action and sins of attitude. Jesus was as concerned about what a man thought in his heart as He was about what the man did. The interpretation of a spiritual dream will always lead both the dreamer and any others the message is shared with into a more holy and pure walk with God. If the message of the dream is more self-serving or speaks to soulish desires, it may not be a spiritual dream.

Does the individual receiving the dream or vision have a personal relationship with the Lord Jesus Christ?

Scripture records instances of God communicating to the unrighteous through dreams and visions. Most often, however, He chooses to communicate with His children. Seldom will God speak anything more than a personal word of admonition to an unbeliever or someone who is not walking in right relationship with Him. Revelation given for the edification of someone else will rarely come from one who does not personally know Christ.

These questions are based on foundations of the Christian faith and provide guidelines by which all revelation must be judged. Those who receive visions must not be so overwhelmed by the experience that they fail to measure the vision by God's standards.

For example, a devout man named Mohammed received visions, supposedly from the angel Gabriel. In these visions, he claimed, the angel called him a prophet—just like Jesus. Jesus was stripped of His deity by this "revelation" and relegated to the same category as Abraham and Moses. Because their message denied Christ, by God's standards these visions must be rejected as false.

Other Leading Indicators of Spiritual Dreams

Other indicators found in Scripture will help you to determine whether God is speaking to you, particularly through dreams, which may be used as flags to get our attention. Since we have been looking to God's Word for our examples, let's return there to examine some of the signals God has sent to get people's attention.

One indication of a spiritual dream may be the *stirring of your spirit* or your emotions upon waking. You may not even directly relate it to what you have just dreamed—you may not remember dreaming at all—but your spirit has been stirred nonetheless.

In the book of Daniel we see that the king had a dream which greatly disturbed him, yet he could not even remember what the dream contained. When this occurs, you may often recall the dream if you lie still and ask God to bring this dream to your remembrance.

Another indication of a spiritual dream could be when a dream you awaken from causes you to *search your soul*, or ask yourself questions, or you may have had questions answered within the context of the dream. Many biblical dreams were soul-searching or directional types of dreams which caused the dreamer to examine his life or direction. The dreams of Jacob are examples of this.

God's voice can be heard even in simple dreams.

Yet another determining factor may be the *repetition of a dream* or having similar dreams. A scriptural example of this occurring is Joseph's two parallel dreams: one in which the sun, the moon and 11 stars bow down to him; the other in which his brother's sheaves of grain bow down to his (see Genesis 37:6-10). Later, in Genesis 41, Pharaoh also has two very similar dreams which the Lord uses to get his attention.

Jesus often used similar parables to expound on a topic to more clearly communicate His point. Similarly, a dream may be repeated or a similar dream brought forth to gain our attention or to emphasize a point. Recurring dreams should be carefully logged and analyzed to reveal the divine message behind them. The message contained therein could very possibly hold an important key to the dreamer's life and circumstances.

While all of the above factors may help you to recognize a spiritual dream, you must always be ready to listen to any dream you receive. Many times God will give you a dream that seems unimportant and of no consequence. However, these can often be of great significance. In order to be diligent to receive and interpret dreams and visions, we must recognize that even in simple dreams God's voice can be heard.

Spiritual Visions Come in Various Forms

Visions are communicated and experienced in many ways. Divine or angelic appearances, trancelike visions, perceiving the future or the spiritual realm with the natural eye or with the eyes of the spirit within an individual are some of the different ways God gives visions.

Balaam was an Old Testament prophet described as the man who "saw the vision of the Almighty, falling into a trance, but having his eyes open" (Numbers 24:4, *KJV*).

Peter fell into a trance when he received the vision of the sheet being lowered from heaven. This vision seemed contrary to all that he had been taught under the Law; however, God spoke to Peter three times within the vision until Peter got the message. The result of this vision was that Peter took the gospel to the Gentiles for the first time (see Acts 10:9-16).

Falling into a trance is not necessary, however, for one to have a vision. As Stephen was being stoned, he saw heaven opened and Jesus standing at the right hand of God (see Acts 7:55). Cornelius had a vision while he was praying and saw the angel of the Lord, who instructed him to send for Peter in Joppa (see Acts 10:1-6). When Jesus first set eyes on Nathaniel, He told Nathaniel that He had "seen" him sitting under a fig tree. How did Jesus have this vision of Nathaniel? Probably by seeing him through the eyes of His Spirit (see John 1:48).

Visions may come in many ways; but it is always important to judge the revelation from the vision based, not on the experience, but according to God's Word, for Satan himself can appear to us as an angel of light (see 2 Corinthians 11:14).

The Value of Soulish Dreams

Of course, soulish, or natural, dreams are not to be ignored, for our own souls can show us things about ourselves that we may otherwise fail to see when awake.

During the process of learning about dreams, it is wise to write down all your dreams so you can better discern between those which are spiritually based and those which are soulish in nature. Then as you learn to interpret that which you've dreamed, you will find it becomes easier to identify the source of your dreams.

Chapter 7

DREAMS REVEAL
THE HEART

The heart is deceitful above all things,
and desperately wicked; who can know it?

JEREMIAH 17:9

One of the primary functions of spiritual dreams is to speak to the issues of the human heart. Dreams are used by God to address areas of spiritual weakness in our lives, as well as areas where we may need emotional healing. Dreams may cause us to look beyond our preconceived ideas of who we are to make an honest assessment of our hearts' condition.

The Lord searches our hearts and knows what is within us. Most of us don't really know the deep thoughts and intentions of our own hearts; therefore we must rely upon the Spirit of God to try, to prove and to reveal that which is within us.

God is continuously drawing us into a place of recognizing those things which may be in our hearts and on our minds that are not in keeping with His ways and His principles. His Word clearly tells us that our ways are not His ways; neither are our thoughts His thoughts (see Isaiah 55:8). God's desire is to communicate with us, to reveal our own thoughts to us, without all the walls of defense or deception that we build around ourselves as a form of protection by the light of day.

David prayed:

Search me, O God, and know my heart;
Try me, and know my anxieties;
And see if there is any wicked way in me,
And lead me in the way everlasting
(Psalm 139:23,24).

This must be the prayer of every saint who strives to walk holy before the Lord. In order to have our hearts and consciences purged and made pure, we must learn to be honest with ourselves—and with God—about our shortcomings, our sins and our selective blind spots. We must allow God to expose what is on the inside, that it might be properly dealt with through repentance, prayer and commitment to change.

Dreams Bypass Our Walls of Self-Defense

Because dreams are produced through our subconscious minds, they will normally bypass our various self-defense mechanisms and preconceived notions about our strengths and weaknesses and go right to the truth of the matter. A personal example of this is a dream I had several years ago. Now, I am a pastor's wife and very much involved in ministry, and I felt that everything in my life was pretty much in order until with the following dream God revealed in me certain weak areas:

The House and the Pond

The dream began with my seeing a big, beautiful two-story house. As I walked in the front door, it was readily apparent that the house was expensively decorated and neat as a pin. Yet as I began to walk down the back hallway, the house began to grow darker and darker. I found some rooms with the doors closed. As I opened one and then the other, I was terrified by what I found in the rooms: darkness and sin. I went running out of the house in fear. As I stumbled breathless onto the front porch, I saw my small four-year-old son standing next to a busy road. He was teasing me, acting like he was going to run out into the middle of the road. I yelled, "Come back!" but he continued his taunting. Then he ran away from the road and skittered onto a frozen pond. I followed, chasing him out to the middle of the pond, where the ice began to crack. The next thing I knew, the ice had broken completely and I was being swallowed up by the icy waters. Then I woke up.

This was a very disturbing dream, but I immediately knew that the Lord was desiring to speak something to me through it. As I prayed and asked the Lord the meaning of the dream, I sensed that His response was "If I show you what it means, you will be responsible for changing certain areas of your life. Will you be obedient?" Not knowing what the specific areas of change were to be, I had to stop and think for a moment. Was I willing to sign the bottom of the contract and then leave the fine print for Him to fill in later? I know my Father intends only good for me, so I replied, "I will." This is the interpretation of this dream:

The house represented me. On the outside it looked well cared for. On the inside, most of the front rooms looked inviting, comfortable and well furnished. But as I explored the house further, God showed me areas of my life that I had not allowed Him to clean up—"rooms" that were dark and frightening. These were parts of my life that no one else saw, that I had refused to yield to His touch. Then, as I ran out of the house and saw my son by the road, God impressed upon me that my child represented the immature portions in my life where I had refused to grow up. If you remember, my son was flirting with danger by the road. This is what these areas of immaturity were causing me to do in my own life. As I reflected on the part of the dream in which I ran after my son onto the pond and we both fell in, I realized that if I were to pursue or chase after these immature areas of my life, the end would be destruction.

Of course, this is a very personal dream; but I share it with you to demonstrate how God can show us the true motives, intentions and conditions of our hearts through our dreams. If any man or woman of God whom I greatly respect had shared with me these very convicting truths about my life, I may not have received their words because of pride or faulty self-perception. However, because this was something that I discovered myself through prayerfully considering my dream, the interpretation of that dream was difficult to deny.

So I repented of closing off these areas of my life to the Lord, and I prayed for God's grace to help me continue to change that I might be more pleasing in His sight.

Job's Understanding of Dreams

The Bible speaks of God's dealing with the hearts of men through dreams. We see in Job that even when God speaks repeatedly to us during our waking hours, we may still not perceive His voice. So it is through dreams that God often must accomplish His purposes:

> Why do you contend with Him? For He does not give an accounting of any of His words. For God may speak in one way, or in another, yet man does not perceive it. In a dream, in a vision of the night, when deep sleep falls upon men, while slumbering on their beds, then He opens the ears of men, and seals their instruction. In order to turn man from his deed, and conceal pride from man, He keeps back his soul from the Pit, and his life from perishing by the sword (Job 33:13-18).

This passage is rich with information concerning the function of dreams as used by God. Set in context, Job had been complaining to God that he had been kept in the dark concerning the meaning of His dealings with him and was therefore convinced that God was dealing with him as He would deal with an enemy. But Job's friend Elihu tells him that God had, in fact, been speaking to him all along; but Job had not been listening.

God is so faithful to His people that He will make repeated attempts to convey His thoughts to us. He will even go so far as to speak through our subconscious minds while we sleep. Let's examine portions of this passage from Job and gain even greater insight.

Visions of the Night

In a dream, in a vision of the night, when deep sleep falls upon men, while slumbering on their beds (Job 33:15).

This verse refers to dreams as visions of the night. As we discussed previously, there is little difference between a dream and a vision—one occurs during sleep and the other usually during waking hours. Dreams occur both during times of deep sleep and times of slumber, or lighter rest. Slumbering would refer to the times early in the night (when you have not yet entered deep-sleep patterns) or right before awakening in the morning.

Some of the most vivid dreams I have had occurred during times of slumber when I have awakened in the morning and decided to sleep "just a little longer." Sleep experts agree that dreams most often remembered occur during these times.

God Uses Dreams to Open Our Ears

Then *He opens the ears of men* and seals their instruction (Job 33:16, emphasis added).

With our busy, hectic schedules, much of the time our ears are not open to hear the voice of God. Although we may feel the Holy Spirit begin to tug at our hearts, we often don't take time out to listen. If we have set aside a quiet time for prayer and meditation on the Word, God may choose to speak to us then through Scripture or with a still, small voice. But He may choose to speak at a time we may not feel is terribly convenient for stopping to fully grasp what He is saying.

As a mother with three small children, I have at times received an answer to prayer or a revelation from the Lord during very noisy, very active moments. To be honest, sometimes I receive what He says completely, while other times (when it seems I can't even hear myself think) it's difficult to get the full impact of His meaning.

In order to fully receive something from God, we must not only be listening for Him but our hearts must be prepared as well. Preparing our hearts to receive Him enables us to be not only hearers but also doers of His will.

During our dreams, God bypasses the shell that often surrounds our hearts and makes us dull of hearing. Dreams give us ears to hear what the Spirit is saying. However, we must consciously alert our minds that the Spirit may indeed be speaking during our sleep. Bible commentator Adam Clarke described it this way:

> A dream or a vision simply considered is likely to do no good; it is the opening of the understanding and the pouring in of the light that make men wise to salvation.[1]

We must open our hearts as well as our ears in order to fully obtain revelation through dreams.

God Uses Dreams to Bring Instruction

Then He opens the ears of men *and seals their instruction* (Job 33:16, emphasis added).

The Hebrew word here for instruction is *mocar*, which is interpreted in the Old Testament as both "instruction" and "admonition." *Webster's Dictionary* defines admonition as "the act of warning or notifying of a fault, to reprove with mildness, to counsel against wrong practices; to caution, advise, or exhort; to instruct or direct; to remind; to recall or urge to duty." God instructs in all these ways in dreams and imprints upon the soul deep and lasting impressions, much the same way a seal and wax are used to make an imprint upon a document.

God Uses Dreams to Bypass Pride

In order to turn man from his deed, and conceal pride from man (Job 33:17).

This particular portion of Scripture is especially important in the discussion of dreams that reveal the true condition of the heart. Pride often cloaks the sinful intentions and evil purposes of our hearts. When we hide behind our pride, we fall prey to self-deception.

When God strips this pride away, we must face the things inside of us that are ungodly, immature, even sinful. When we dream, our hearts may plead with us to do that which is right and to turn from our evil ways. Strive as we might to do good during our waking hours, we may learn during our sleep that although we have not given in to temptation, in our hearts there remains a struggle to overcome sin.

Dreams are formed from thoughts and images in our minds, often showing us sin that may be present in our hearts but which our conscious minds have refused to acknowledge. God desires that we be dead to sin and that sin should not reign in our mortal bodies. We are not to be conformed to the ways of the flesh but to be transformed by the renewing of our minds, both conscious and subconscious (see Romans 12:2).

Even the apostle Paul experienced the battle between the carnal, fleshly mind and the spirit (see Romans 7:18-23). Today, we are ever engaged in the same battle. Dreams often reveal areas of struggle within us—areas of weakness or imperfection where the enemy may attempt to catch us unaware.

While we are on the earth, each of us continues in God's perfecting process (see Philippians 1:6). Don't be fooled into thinking, *If there were sin in my heart, I would know about it.* God's Word tells us the heart is deceitful. Therefore, we must allow Him to continuously search us for "any wicked way" and lead us "in the way everlasting" (Psalm 139:24).

Convicted but Not Condemned

The purpose of God's revealing our sin and weaknesses to us through our dreams is to draw us into closer communion with Him. Our dreams should not become a source of condemnation but should prompt us to seek to understand what God is saying to us. When we feel convicted in our spirits of sin, God's intention is not to leave us in a helpless and hopeless state but to bring us to a place of repentance. "If we confess our sins, He is faithful and just to forgive us our sins and to cleanse us from all unrighteousness" (1 John 1:9).

Dreams often reveal areas of struggle within us.

Nebuchadnezzar's Dream

In the book of Daniel, we find the story of King Nebuchadnezzar and his disturbing dreams. The king of the great nation of Babylon awoke one night from a dream that troubled his spirit— a dream he could not remember.

So Nebuchadnezzar sent for the magicians, sorcerers and astrologers of his court and demanded that they tell him his dream and, while they were at it, to provide an interpretation. The royal advisers protested that they would be happy to tell the interpretation to the dream if the king would just share it with them. Knowing, however, that his wise men were not above speaking "lying and corrupt words" (Daniel 2:9) to mollify him, the king demanded that they tell him his dream, then interpret it. "And by the way," the king added, "if you cannot do this, I will have you all killed!" No pressure.

There was in the king's court a young man of Judah who, though a captive in the land of Babylon, had gained favor and goodwill in the court because he remained faithful to the God of his fathers. Daniel was considered a wise man in the kingdom and would have suffered the same fate as the magicians had he not prayed and asked the Lord to give him the king's dream and its interpretation. The Lord was faithful to answer him and gave Daniel a night vision. In other words, Daniel dreamed the same dream the king had. When he approached the king, he told Nebuchadnezzar that only God in heaven would reveal these secret things to him:

> The secret which the king has demanded, the wise men, the astrologers, the magicians, and the soothsayers cannot declare to the king. But there is a God in heaven who reveals secrets, and He has made known to King

Nebuchadnezzar what will be in the latter days. Your dream, and the visions of your head upon your bed, were these: As for you, O king, thoughts came to your mind while on your bed, about what would come to pass after this; and He who reveals secrets has made known to you what will be. But as for me, this secret has not been revealed to me because I have more wisdom than anyone living, but for our sakes who make known the interpretation to the king, and that you may know the thoughts of your heart (Daniel 2:27-30).

Daniel went on to give the king the dream and the interpretation, which prophesied about Nebuchadnezzar's kingdom and a greater kingdom to come. The king was so excited by this revelation that he fell on his face before Daniel and declared his God to be "the God of gods" (v. 47). Then he honored Daniel and made him a wealthy ruler over the province.

But the king did not heed the dream's warning and, as so many do after the thrill of an exciting spiritual experience wears off, Nebuchadnezzar returned to his ways of sin. The next chapter finds Nebuchadnezzar erecting a statue in his own honor and when three of Daniel's friends refuse to bow before it, he throws them, bound, into a fiery furnace. Once again, he has an encounter with God as he sees not three, but four men walking around unharmed in the midst of the flames. He brings the young men of Judah out of the fire and declares their God to be superior to all other gods.

Once again, God began to deal with Nebuchadnezzar, as God will often speak more than once to get His point across. The king had another vision which frightened him, and again he called for his astrologers, magicians and soothsayers. Again they could not tell him the meaning of his dream, so Daniel was summoned.

The king described his vision to Daniel, who hesitated to give Nebuchadnezzar the bad news. Daniel told the Babylonian king that the Lord would cause him to be driven from his throne and into the fields, where he would live with the beasts and eat grass like the oxen—until Nebuchadnezzar recognized that the Most High rules the kingdom of men and that He gives reign to whomever He chooses. So Daniel counseled the king:

> Therefore, O king, let my advice be acceptable to you; *break off your sins by being righteous,* and your iniquities by showing mercy to the poor. Perhaps there may be a lengthening of your prosperity (Daniel 4:27, emphasis added).

In the face of such a dire prophecy, you would think the king would do whatever was necessary to ensure that this calamity did not befall him. Yet just one year later the king walked into the palace and began boasting of how *he* had built this great Babylon by the might of *his* power and for the honor of *his* majesty. While the words were still in his mouth, a voice thundered from heaven, saying:

> King Nebuchadnezzar, to you it is spoken: the kingdom has departed from you! (Daniel 4:31).

God then drove the great king away from men and into the fields, where he ate grass as the oxen and where his body became wet with dew from sleeping on the ground. His hair grew "like eagles' feathers" and his nails "like birds' claws" (v. 33).

The Dream Revealed the Heart of the King

God's message to Nebuchadnezzar was conveyed through dreams that disturbed him. Though he did not understand what the dreams were saying, the king knew there was a significant message contained within them. God was dealing with his heart and instructing him in the ways of repentance.

God will deal with us in the same manner at times by giving us dreams which we may not understand but that disturb our peace of mind. When this happens, the dream should be interpreted and a godly response given.

Had the king heeded the warnings given both by his dream and by Daniel, he would not have found himself in such a desolate condition. The great ruler of Babylon had become an outcast because he refused to turn from his pride and idolatry.

Many a great man down through history has been destroyed for the same reasons. Failure to repent, failure to acknowledge God, stubbornness, pride and wickedness all contributed to mankind's sad state.

God's Spirit Leads Men to Repentance

After a length of time, Nebuchadnezzar's understanding returned and he realized the error of his ways. He finally acknowledged God and blessed Him and praised Him as the ruler of the everlasting dominion. He was then restored to his place of honor as king. From his throne he proclaimed:

Now I, Nebuchadnezzar, praise and extol and honor the King of heaven, all of whose works are truth, and His ways justice. And those who walk in *pride* He is able to put down (Daniel 4:37, emphasis added).

God did what was necessary to get Nebuchadnezzar's attention, beginning with dreams and their interpretations and proceeding to judgment when repentance was not forthcoming. In the end, the king repented and gained spiritual understanding.

Daniel Knew God's Voice

Daniel was God's prophet, His spokesman to the great Nebuchadnezzar. Daniel had a gift for interpreting dreams which, had the king listened and responded appropriately, would have spared the king much heartache. Daniel interpreted dreams through God's enablement, much the same way as a prophecy or a word of knowledge is received from the Lord. The Holy Spirit revealed the dreams to him and provided their interpretation.

Daniel was able to interpret dreams because he had learned to listen to and trust the voice of God. While someone may have a natural ability to dissect and analyze spiritual dreams, scriptural dream interpretation is only possible as one is able to hear and understand God's voice.

Daniel prayed to the Lord several times each day, so he knew the Lord's voice when, under threat of death, he was forced to interpret the king's dream. Knowing God and His voice are imperative if you desire to receive the full benefit of your dreams.

God was able to use Daniel in this important role because the young man had purposed in his heart to be a man of integrity and holiness, even in the midst of a corrupt pagan culture. He and his friends did not allow themselves to be defiled by the ways of Babylon; they kept themselves pure. Because of their dedication to serving their God, the Lord chose to bless these four young men: "God gave them knowledge and skill in all literature and wisdom; and Daniel had understanding in all visions and dreams" (Daniel 1:17).

Daniel's gifting clearly came from God. Magicians and astrologers with their occultic powers could not give the king the interpretation he sought. Even today, those who boast of psychic powers and the ability to interpret dreams cannot give accurate revelation apart from the power of the Holy Spirit.

Daniel was gifted by the one true God. Through hearing God's voice, he was able to speak revelation concerning the lives of rulers of four kingdoms: Babylon, the Medo-Persian kingdom, the Grecian kingdom and the Roman kingdom. God's divine gifting gave him favor and insight to affect entire nations.

In these last days, as God pours His Spirit out on all flesh and godly men and women learn to hear God's voice through dreams and visions, the destiny of entire nations may once again be affected by the word of the Lord that brings life!

Note
1. Matthew Henry, et. al., *The Bethany Parallel Commentary of the Old Testament* (Minneapolis, MN: Bethany House Publishers, 1985), p. 940.

Chapter 8

DREAMS OF ENCOURAGEMENT

God shall supply all your need according to
His riches in glory by Christ Jesus.

PHILIPPIANS 4:19

My husband and I were once given great comfort and encouragement by way of a vision that came to a woman whom we had never before met. This woman, who lived 45 miles away, was praying in her living room one afternoon when suddenly the image of a baby dropped into the middle of the room and hung suspended in the air. She could not see the baby's face, but she thought it was odd that both the baby's hands and feet were covered by socks. She prayed for the baby but did not understand the vision—that is, until later on that week.

I had just given birth to a son with a facial birth defect. The area of his defect was so sensitive that we had to keep socks on his hands to keep him from harming himself. We dedicated him to the Lord during one of our Friday night services when the woman who had experienced the vision happened to be visiting our church. When the baby was held up to the Lord in dedication, she realized that my son was the baby who had appeared in her living room.

God had used the vision to inspire this woman to organize prayer for my son during the early days of infancy and corrective surgery. We knew that the Lord had been watching over us and our child; but when we learned of this woman's vision and her prayers, we were blessed with a tremendous amount of fresh encouragement and hope during a very traumatic season in our lives.

Exhortation from Revelation

The Lord our God cares about everything that affects and influences the lives of His children. His desire is to meet all our needs according to His great riches. Too often, however, we have our own ideas about how God can best meet our specific needs.

When, during a time of struggle, we do not receive the answer we expect or if the answer has been long in coming, we may begin to lose hope, become discouraged or even doubt whether God will answer at all. During such a time, God may speak to us through a dream or vision to exhort and encourage us.

God often spoke to the needs of men and women in the Scriptures for the purpose of bringing comfort and hope through revelation. Let's look at several of these and how God used dreams or visions to speak to their needs.

Abraham: A Future and Heritage Revealed

Abraham was a wealthy man of his day. He owned much cattle, silver and gold, but something was missing. He had no children, no heir to whom he would leave his wealth upon his death, for his wife was barren. But Abraham was a man of God, and the Lord appeared unto Abraham in a vision and promised to him an heir, a child of his own. He then told Abraham that his descendants would be as many as the stars in the sky. And

Abraham believed God and the Lord credited it to him as righteousness (see Genesis 15:1-6).

That evening Abraham fell into a deep sleep, and the Lord showed him things concerning the future of the nation of people (Israel) that would be descended from him. The Lord told of how they would be enslaved in cruel bondage to another nation (Egypt) for 400 years, but the Lord would deliver them and they would come out with great possessions and return to that land He had promised to Abraham. The dream also revealed that Abraham would live long and die in peace at an old age (see vv. 12-16).

That same day, the Lord made a covenant with Abraham to give the land "from the river of Egypt to the great river, the River Euphrates," to Abraham and his seed (v. 18). Though for a time his descendants would be slaves, God provided a promise that Abraham's seed would return and claim the land on which Abraham stood as their rightful possession. This was God's prophetic promise to Abraham through a dream.

The birth and destiny of an entire nation was revealed in a vision and a dream and came to fruition because Abraham believed the word of the Lord. Abraham had longed for an heir and God spoke to his need far beyond his expectations. At times, the promises we receive from God may be generational prophecies that our children and their children will bring to complete fulfillment. Prophecies to individuals may require a lifetime to fulfill, while prophecies to families may require an entire generation. Prophecies to nations may be fulfilled over many centuries.

Jacob: Strategy for Prosperity Revealed

In Genesis 28 we find Abraham's grandson Jacob on his way to the house of Laban to take a wife. Through trickery, Jacob had stolen the birthright of his elder brother Esau and obtained the blessings normally given to the firstborn. Esau sought to kill him for his deceit so Jacob's mother, Rebekah, sent him away to seek a wife in the land of her brother Laban. On the way, Jacob stopped for the night and as he slept, he dreamed:

> He dreamed, and behold, a ladder was set up on the earth, and its top reached to heaven; and there the angels of God were ascending and descending on it. And behold, the LORD stood above it and said: "I am the LORD God of Abraham your father and the God of Isaac; the land on which you lie I will give to you and your descendants" (Genesis 28:12,13).

The Lord went on to assure Jacob that He would be with him wherever he would go and that He would bring Jacob back to the land that He had promised to him (see v. 15).

Two wives and 11 sons later, God spoke again to Jacob in a dream (see Genesis 31:10-13). For many years, Jacob had been working for his father-in-law, Laban, who had been cheating him all that time. In the dream, God revealed to Jacob a plan for dividing fairly the cattle of Laban's flocks and taking his rightful portion for himself. (This is the first recorded instance of God imparting sound business strategy and financial advice through a dream.) God also used this dream to tell Jacob to take his wives, his children and his flocks and return to the land of his father.

Jacob, whose name meant "supplanter," had stolen his birthright; but actually receiving the blessing of the Lord was a long and arduous process as God allowed Jacob to be dealt with deceitfully by Laban. Through a dream, God's promise had been given; and through God's purging process, the promise was fulfilled and Jacob became Israel, meaning "prince with God" (see Genesis 32:28).

Dreams will often challenge us to change just as Jacob was challenged to change. Just because God did not directly address Jacob's character flaws in his dreams did not mean that God approved of all that happened in Jacob's life. Similarly, when we receive a word from the Lord, whether through prophecy, dream or vision, we must know that the outcome of His word will depend on our obedient cooperation with God's processes of maturing and purging in our lives.

Joseph: Future Ministry Revealed

Joseph was a young man of 17 when he had two dreams which seemed to do nothing but get him in trouble. Of all Jacob's 12 children, Joseph was the most loved and favored by his father. As a result, the 10 older brothers grew intensely jealous; they hated Joseph and "could not speak peaceably to him" (Genesis 37:4).

The strife in Jacob's household was exacerbated when young Joseph had two dreams—one in which his brother's sheaves bowed down to his sheaf, and the other in which the sun, the moon and 11 stars bowed down to him. Joseph shared these dreams with his brothers and, perhaps understandably, his brothers hated him all the more. Even his father rebuked him, although he took heed of what Joseph had said (see Genesis 37:5-11).

When Joseph shared these dreams with his brothers, he did not do so out of pride or boasting but perhaps with more zeal than wisdom. His brothers became so outraged that, while in the fields tending their flocks, they sold their dreaming brother into slavery to a caravan traveling to Egypt. Joseph served many years in slavery and even spent time in an Egyptian prison, although the Lord used these events to put him in a position of power where his dreams were fulfilled.

Prayerful consideration should be given concerning whether our dreams should be shared and with whom. Much chaos and unnecessary turmoil can be avoided if we will only act in wisdom. Paul prayed for the Christians at Ephesus that God would give them wisdom in addition to revelation (see Ephesians 1:17). Revelation without wisdom can cause great heartache and pain; both must be utilized in proper balance to accomplish God's ultimate purposes.

Joseph's dreams were not particularly difficult to interpret—even his thick-headed, hard-hearted brothers knew what they meant. Perhaps Joseph was unwise to share these dreams with his already jealous siblings. Nevertheless, God orchestrated the ensuing events to providentially thrust Joseph into God's plans for the destiny of Egypt and, eventually, the children of Israel.

So what purpose did the dreams themselves serve? God's promise of greatness given through the dreams gave Joseph hope, guidance and encouragement which kept him from forsaking the God of his fathers during difficult times. Joseph's faithfulness to follow the ways of God was key to his success.

Because Joseph remained faithful through times of testing and trial, God remained faithful to Joseph and brought his dreams to pass. Pharaoh made Joseph prime minister over the land of Egypt, and Joseph saw the country through seven years of famine. When Joseph's brothers came to Egypt for provisions, they bowed before him just as the dreams foretold.

God may have been speaking to Joseph's need for being accepted and loved by his brothers through these same dreams, but God had much more in mind. God had a destiny for Joseph that would be fulfilled only after many years of hardship and faithfulness.

Dreams and visions may reveal your future ministry and destiny; but they rarely reveal the process God will use to bring their fulfillment.

Joseph may have been unwise in sharing his dreams, but he properly responded to God's promise by remaining faithful to Him even in a strange land and under trying circumstances. God remained faithful to Joseph and, in His time, fulfilled His word and brought these dreams to pass, saving not only Joseph and his family but also the future nation of Israel.

Dreams may reveal your destiny; but they rarely reveal the process God will use to fulfill that destiny.

Gideon:
Assurance of Victory Given

Gideon was encouraged by a dream that was dreamed by an enemy soldier. The dream and its interpretation were given to bolster Gideon's faith as he was preparing according to the instructions of the Lord to lead a mere 300 Israelites into battle against a multitude. God directed him to go and listen to what the men in the enemy ranks were saying on the eve of battle. There, Gideon overheard one man talking to another about his dream:

And when Gideon had come, there was a man telling a dream to his companion. He said, "I have had a dream: To my surprise, a loaf of barley bread tumbled into the camp of Midian; it came to a tent and struck it so that it fell and overturned, and the tent collapsed."

Then his companion answered and said, "This is nothing else but the sword of Gideon the son of Joash, a man of Israel! Into his hand God has delivered Midian and the whole camp."

And so it was, when Gideon heard the telling of the dream and its interpretation, that he worshiped. He returned to the camp of Israel, and said, "Arise, for the LORD has delivered the camp of Midian into your hand" (Judges 7:13-15).

This dream ministered directly to Gideon's need for confidence to enter into warfare with the Midianites. He faithfully responded to the encouragement of the Lord by first worshiping the Lord and then returning to his outnumbered troops and declaring that the Lord had already delivered the armies of Midian into their hands. This declaration gave Israel the boldness and courage needed to follow Gideon into battle with his unconventional weapons of warfare (trumpets, pitchers and lamps) and utterly destroy their enemies.

As with dreams God may give today, this dream imparted confidence in God's ability to bring victory in difficult situations. If we seek Him, God will always give us hope and courage when we face battles, whether they are inner conflicts or spiritual warfare. He may use your dreams to provide a vision of the victory or to instill confidence in His ability to triumph in your situation.

Solomon: Wisdom Given and Desires Granted

Solomon was crowned king of Israel after the death of his father, King David. Solomon loved God with all his heart, but he was young and lacked confidence in his ability to rule the people. While Solomon was in Gibeon, the Lord appeared to him in a dream and said, "Ask! What shall I give you?" (1 Kings 3:5).

Young Solomon could have asked for anything—long life, fabulous riches, great power. Instead he humbly asked for the wisdom to discern between good and evil that he might properly judge the people of Israel. Solomon's request pleased the Lord, and God released to him a measure of wisdom so great that the world has not seen the equivalent since that time.

God had seen the heart cry of His servant, and He spoke and released His anointing through a dream. Thereafter, Solomon ruled with confidence and wisdom; and long life, fabulous riches and great power were added to him. When the Lord uses our dreams to speak to an area of need in our lives, there may come an impartation of God's Spirit which releases such power and revelation as to vastly alter our character and abilities.

From these biblical examples we see that God will often identify a need in our lives, minister a word or message in regard to that need and then await our response. For some of these great men of God, their needs were not immediately met; however, the promises contained within their dreams gave them determination to press past difficult circumstances and persevere until the promises were fulfilled.

Dreams Can Release Rejoicing

While my husband and I were building a new home, I experienced some anxiety regarding the money needed to make certain changes we had requested during construction. The most costly change involved putting a tile roof on the house rather than one made of asphalt. As my faith was undergoing a bit of stretching, I had the following dream:

The Tarantula Roof

Everyone was excited because we were putting on our new tile roof. The excitement stemmed from the fact that the tiles were made of a new and innovative and costly material—the very best! The tiles were made from the dried, preserved bodies of *tarantula spiders*. Frankly, I was having a tough time seeing what was so exciting about these strange tiles. Then I found myself going into the homes of people I knew, and I saw they were raising baby tarantulas with great joy and excitement. They were feeding them, putting them to bed, etc. Again, this did not seem normal but was very strange to me.

When I awoke, I was perplexed by this dream and thought, *Surely this can't have an edifying meaning. Everyone knows spiders are evil.* All day, the dream stayed with me; and late that night I lay in bed, praying and pondering the dream.

I decided to get out of bed and look up "tarantula" in the encyclopedia. This is what the entry said:

In the Middle Ages it was believed that people bitten by the tarantula spider became ill with *tarantism*. In the disease, which was superstition, the victim developed a strong desire to dance![1]

The encyclopedia went on to say that this dance, the disease and the spider were all named after a town in Italy called Taranto—

which, oddly enough, called to mind the Canadian city of Toronto, where there had been a highly publicized outpouring of joy among God's people. I also learned that the bite of the tarantula is actually not harmful to humans and that the tarantula is the only spider that aggressively chases down its prey instead of waiting for food to become trapped in its web.

The Lord used my dream to say that He was going to cover our home with joy and rejoicing, which was symbolized, strangely enough, by a tarantula. As people fear the spider's bite without cause, so I was acting in fear instead of faith. God was assuring me that my worry was groundless because He would provide us with joy and abundance.

In my dream, the spiders were also being raised in the homes of our church members. God was encouraging me with the promise that His joy would be poured out in every home in our congregation and that it would produce a boldness to go forth in His name and destroy the strongholds of the enemy.

When the interpretation finally came, I was overcome with joy and laughter and was full of faith. Who would ever guess that a tarantula would cause rejoicing?!

Dreams and Emotional Healing

Since dreams may reveal what is within our hearts, certain emotional issues that have been suppressed or otherwise ignored in our conscious thinking may be brought out in our dreams. Dreams will often remind us of these unresolved matters of the heart and encourage us to deal with them so that we may be whole.

Although consciously you may feel that certain events from your past have been dealt with sufficiently, your subconscious mind will often recognize when things have been left undone and will remind you through dreams that healing or even simple acknowledgment must take place. By bringing such matters to mind, God calls our attention to the need for healing and begins the healing process.

Often we build walls around areas of emotional pain to shield us from the hurt. God will use dreams to bypass these walls to go directly to the source of the pain.

A man who had lost several close family members in different ways in a short period of time came to me, saying he was dreaming about these loved ones every night. Consciously, he felt that he had accepted their deaths and was bothered by the recurrence of these dreams. I asked whether he had ever allowed himself to grieve over his loss or if he constantly felt he had to keep up a good front and be strong for others who were grieving. He thought about this a moment and replied that he had never really dealt with his own grief. I prayed with him and we asked the Lord to help and encourage him during his grieving process. From that night forward the dreams ceased.

What this man's conscious mind had not allowed him to feel or deal with, his subconscious mind would not let him forget. God spoke to his need through his dreams and prompted him to seek the Lord for emotional healing.

Note
1. "Tarantula," *Encyclopedia Brittanica*, vol. T-V (1971), p. 168.

Chapter 9

WARNING AND DIRECTION FROM DREAMS AND VISIONS

Your word is a lamp to my feet and a light to my path.

PSALM 119:105

Often when we are seeking the direction of the Lord for our lives, the Lord will speak to us in our sleep or through images and pictures when we are awake. His Word promises, "The steps of a good man are ordered by the LORD" (Psalm 37:23).

We may at times stray from the correct path because we do not fully comprehend God's ways or His plans for our lives, but God will find a way to speak to us if our hearts are sincerely seeking to do what is right in the sight of the Lord. God will always find a way to speak to His people when we need direction—or a warning.

Dreams and Visions of Warning

In dreams of divine warning, God may direct us to do something—or not to do something—in order to protect us from a danger that we may not be able to see or discern. Often such dreams are dismissed as fantasy or fear, when in actuality God is speaking and directing us to take action.

We must use discernment to interpret such dreams and act on revelation where it exists, but we must not allow ourselves to become paranoid, reading danger into every dream we have. To do so would emotionally cripple us and place us in bondage. As you learn to discern God's voice, you will learn to clearly recognize warnings when they are given.

Once we discern that God is warning us of impending danger, we must yield ourselves to prayer to cut off the intended evil. Just because you dream something frightening, something you feel is a warning of things to come, does not mean that thing has to occur. Many times in Scripture, God seemed to have made up his mind to rain judgment upon a people for their disobedience, until a man of God interceded on their behalf and prayed that God would show mercy and His hand of judgment was stayed (see Numbers 14:11-20, for example).

We must remain sensitive, however, allowing the Holy Spirit to direct us how to pray in these situations. For example, many Christians have seen the death of a loved one in a dream. This could mean that God would have us pray for protection to divert the plan of death, or it could be God warning and preparing us emotionally for a loss He has already determined will occur. Or it could have an entirely different meaning altogether, such as speaking of the death of a part of ourselves, or perhaps God is planning to do something new in our natural relationships.

The Wise Men's Dream

Matthew 2:1-12 tells the story of the Magi—wise men from the East who sought the newborn King, that they might worship Him and bring Him gifts. Herod, the wicked ruler of Judea, tried to trick the Magi into revealing the place of this new King's birth so that he might destroy the child. With input from the chief priests and scribes and with the help of a mysterious moving star, the Magi found Jesus and set before Him gifts of gold, frankincense and myrrh.

But before they returned to their homeland, God warned them in a dream that they should not return to Herod, for he sought to take the child's life. Therefore, the wise men departed and went a different way back to their own country (see Matthew 2:12). Young Jesus was spared from Herod's murderous treachery because the Magi obeyed the direction of the Lord given through a dream.

Joseph's Dream Home

Being sensitive to the direction of God concerning a place to live and the timing of their move, Joseph did not return immediately to Nazareth from Bethlehem; instead he took his family to Egypt:

> Behold, the angel of the Lord appeared to Joseph in a dream saying, "Arise and take the young Child and His mother, flee to Egypt, and stay there until I bring you word; for Herod will seek the young Child to destroy Him" (Matthew 2:13).

The angel of the Lord instructed Joseph through a dream to arise and take his family into Egypt until God brought him further word. Joseph obeyed, enabling the prophecy in Hosea to be fulfilled: "Out of Egypt I called My Son" (Matthew 2:15).

The young family was again uprooted when the angel appeared once more to Joseph and told him that Herod had died and it was time to return to the land of Israel (vv. 19,20).

During the journey, Joseph heard the news that Herod's son was reigning in Judea and he feared for his son's life. But the angel appeared to Joseph in yet another dream and instructed him to settle in Galilee.

Being warned by God in a dream, he turned aside into the region of Galilee. And he came and dwelt in a city called Nazareth, that it might be fulfilled which was spoken by the prophets, "He shall be called a Nazarene" (Matthew 2:22,23).

Each of these moves was made according to the direction and timing of the Lord.

Do not dismiss casually a dream or vision you perceive to be a warning.

Abraham Lincoln's Dream

We must be sure to heed dreams or visions we perceive as warnings and not dismiss them casually. Such a dream was given to Abraham Lincoln the night prior to his assassination. In his dream, he saw himself descending a staircase and entering a room where he saw a casket surrounded by guards. When he asked what was happening, someone told him that the president had been shot. After awaking from this startling dream, he had a vision of himself in a boat taking a long journey to a distant shore.

Yet when it came time to go to the theater on that next fateful night, he shunned his bodyguard's protection and inadvertently put himself in the path of an assassin's bullet. Had he regarded his dream as a warning, he may have taken extra precautions and avoided a premature death.

Vision of the House in Flames

I once had a vision of my house going up in flames. I didn't react in fear, but I did pray and ask that any evil planned for my house or my household would be diverted. I didn't give the vision a second thought after that time.

Three days later, while changing a lightbulb in my son's bedroom, I found a sock that had apparently been thrown into the lamp shade and had burned. Had the lightbulb not burned out, this could have started a fire and destroyed the house; but because I heeded the warning given by God, prayerful intervention was made and tragedy was possibly avoided.

Dreams and Visions of Direction

The Lord will at times give direction through dreams and visions. Such was the case 2,000 years ago when the Lord spoke to a carpenter named Joseph, of the lowly village of Nazareth.

Joseph's Dream Concerning Mary

Joseph and Mary were betrothed when Mary was discovered to

be with child. Being a man of honor, Joseph planned to break off the betrothal quietly and privately. But an angel of the Lord appeared to Joseph in a dream and told him not to be afraid to take Mary as his wife, for she was pregnant not with another man's child but with a Son conceived by the Holy Spirit, and they were to name Him Jesus. So Joseph took Mary as his wife and when she bore a Son, they named him Jesus (see Matthew 1:18-25).

Every day, Christians everywhere pray in the mighty name of Jesus. We call upon that name, sing songs magnifying that name and share the good news about that name. There is no other name under heaven whereby men must be saved but by the name of Jesus (see Acts 4:12). And this name was given to the Christ child because of direction given in a dream.

Signposts for the Apostles

The Lord sometimes gave direction to the disciples of the Early Church through the experience of visions.

In Acts 9, a persecutor of the Church, Saul of Tarsus, had a startling encounter with Jesus on the road to Damascus. Saul fell to the ground and was converted on the spot. But when he arose, Saul was blind and had to be led by the hand to Damascus where he remained blind for three days.

Meanwhile, the Lord appeared in a vision to a disciple named Ananias and directed him to go to Saul:

> To him the Lord said in a vision, "Ananias." And he said, "Here I am, Lord." So the Lord said to him, "Arise and go to the street called Straight, and inquire at the house of Judas for one called Saul of Tarsus, for behold, he is praying. And in a vision he has seen a man named

Ananias coming in and putting his hand on him, so that
he might receive his sight" (Acts 9:10-12).

Ananias had heard much about this persecutor of the righteous, and he argued briefly with the Lord. But the Lord told him,
"Go, for he is a chosen vessel of Mine to bear My name before
Gentiles, kings, and the children of Israel. For I will show him
how many things he must suffer for My name's sake" (Acts
9:15,16).

This vision was extremely directive, as was a later vision
given to Saul (now Paul) in which a man from Macedonia said to
him, "Come over to Macedonia and help us" (Acts 16:9).

These are New Testament examples of God's speaking and
directing the specific steps of His followers through dreams and
visions. He continues to speak to men and women today in the
same way, as we earnestly desire to fulfill His will.

Chapter 10

DREAMS AND THE GIFTS OF THE HOLY SPIRIT

Let us pursue the things which make for peace and the things by which one may edify another.

ROMANS 14:19

Pursue love, and desire spiritual gifts. . . . Even so you, since you are zealous for spiritual gifts, let it be for the edification of the church that you seek to excel.

1 CORINTHIANS 14:1,12

Where does the Holy Spirit go when we are asleep? Of course the Holy Spirit does not sleep but abides in us at all times, as do the wonderful gifts He brings. He dwells within us whether we are asleep or awake, manifesting the gifts and callings of God in our lives.

Although dreaming is not one of the nine gifts of the Holy Spirit listed in 1 Corinthians 12, dreams can be a conduit through which some of these spiritual gifts flow. As we have seen, many dreams are inspired by the Holy Spirit, so it is only natural for an individual's spiritual gifts to become evident when he or she dreams. It is important to note that the gifts of the Holy Spirit are given to edify the Church and are generally activated to bless others (see 1 Corinthians 12:7; 14:12).

Therefore, as the gifts of the Spirit operate in dreams, it will not be unusual for the message of a dream to relate to someone other than just the dreamer. Let's look at some examples of how the gifts of revelation may be made manifest in our dreams.

Prophecy

God will often speak to His people concerning future events which are to take place. Though your dreams may be difficult to interpret if they are heavy on symbolism, God may be speaking to you concerning changes or challenges which are to come.

Some people have prophetic dreams or visions with great accuracy of detail, knowing the identity of someone they will meet or places they will go and what is to be said and done in these instances. Those who have the gift of prophecy may have dreams which predict or foretell future events. Abraham, Jacob and the prophet Daniel were given dreams that predicted future events not only for their own lives but also for nations.

Again, if you feel God has spoken prophetically to you about your personal future, always submit the revelation to someone in a position of authority who can counsel you in your interpretation.

Those who eagerly receive every dream as a personal prophecy concerning direction for their future are placing themselves in a dangerous position in which they can easily become deceived by the enemy. We all have blind spots in our lives, so it is wise to allow someone else to evaluate your interpretation of dreams, especially if the dreams are going to influence you in any way to make a major life decision. We are to always act with wisdom when given revelation.

Also, be cautious not to build doctrine around revelation contained in a dream. This is a dangerous trap, one that others have fallen into only to be led into deception.

A Church in Danger

While not all who have the gift of prophecy may dream dreams of national importance, there may come revelations of a corporate nature concerning the future of a local church. The pastor of a large West Coast church once told of having a dream in which a large group of radical demonstrators converged on his church bent on destroying property and harassing church members. The dream concerned him so much that he had a large fence installed around the church grounds. Within months, the church found itself in the midst of political controversy over a citywide prayer meeting concerning the abortion issue. During the evening prayer meetings, hundreds of radicals came to the church to attempt to disrupt their prayer activities. Police were called in to control the crowds, and the fence which had been constructed greatly aided in protecting those praying inside the church. This dream was very literal in its presentation and its fulfillment.

Blizzard In Florida

I once dreamed of a strange winter storm hitting the coast of the panhandle of Florida with blizzardlike conditions. The dream contained great detail which I recorded. Five weeks later in the month of March, an unusual winter storm hit the panhandle of Florida with high winds and snow. I had not realized at the time that the dream was actually foretelling an event.

Shrubbery and Turnip Greens

One man was in the midst of a geographic relocation when he had a dream showing him his new house in detail, all the way down to the shrubbery in the front yard. When he arrived at his new location and began house hunting, he came upon the very house he had seen in his dream—down to the smallest detail. He knew God had spoken to him and that this was the house he was to purchase.

I had a dream once in which I came home and found the grass in my front yard pulled up and turnip greens planted in its place. There were rows and rows of turnip greens! Now, I do *not* like the taste of turnip greens. It doesn't matter how they are cooked; I just don't like them.

The next day after I had this dream, a little old man approached me while I was shopping in town. He shoved a big bunch of greens in my face and said, "Ya wanna buy some turnip greens?" I was taken aback and instantly remembered my dream. A bit shocked, I said, "Thank you, but no, thank you." I immediately went to my car, shut the door and said, "OK, Lord, I get the message. What are you trying to tell me?"

When I asked if this silly little dream had any meaning, God showed me that He was preparing to do a new planting in my life. He was getting ready to pluck up the things that were comfortable and pleasant in my life and replace them with things I may not like but would be good for me.

This began a time of purging and growth in my life. For the next year, God took me through a time when I had to eat my words for all the times I had said "I'll never do this" or "I'll never do that." Every one of those "nevers" tasted like bitter turnip greens to me. But in the end, I had to agree that they were good for me. I was stronger and healthier because of the sometimes painful process God had taken me through. It would have been much more difficult to endure had God not prepared me for it with that little dream.

The House Of Eastern Gods

A woman once brought a dream to me, asking for assistance in interpreting the dream. She had held onto the dream for several years because it was so vivid to her and caused her great concern. In the dream she and her husband were in a house that was apparently theirs. The house had decorations on the walls that resembled the images of Eastern gods. As they sat at a table together, the gods started moving and causing demonstrations of occult power throughout the house, affecting all who dwelled in the house.

As this woman and I talked about some of the different possible meanings of the dream and what some of these events could symbolize, her father commented on the fact that this couple had just moved into a new home. He then reminded his daughter that the previous owners had been deeply involved with Eastern religion and had even left statues and altars in the house when they moved.

The dream was alluding to certain spirits that were evident in the house as a result of the activities of the previous occupants. The couple had had to deal with certain occultic manifestations since moving in but had never associated these problems with her dream of years ago or the activities of the home's previous owners. The dream, when properly interpreted, provided the key to dealing with these lingering spiritual powers.

Words of Knowledge

Revelation beyond any natural knowledge comes through this gift of the Holy Spirit. God is faithful to reveal things that are vital to our spiritual walk when we have needs that supercede our natural limitations.

The Missing Intercessor

One example of the word of knowledge in operation in dreams involved a church that reported the disappearance of one of its young ladies who was active in prayer ministry. One day she left work and never made it home. She had been missing for several days when the pastor called, asking if we would pray about her whereabouts.

That night before going to sleep, I asked the Lord to give me a dream to show me where the young woman was and whether she was alive or dead. As I slept, I dreamed of an old cabin next to a murky river with red clay around it. I did not see the girl in the dream, but when I woke up, I had the feeling she was all right.

I shared the dream the next day with a man who was familiar with the town where the girl lived. He said there was indeed a murky river with red clay banks on the outskirts of town. That afternoon I received a call saying the girl had been kidnaped but escaped and walked back to town unharmed. She told of being held captive by a man in an old wood shack next to a muddy river.

God had given me supernatural insight and information—a word of knowledge—through my dream.

Words of Wisdom

Words of wisdom are words of direction, spiritual instruction or counsel that are prompted by the Spirit of God through divine revelation. As mentioned before, dreams can often be instructional and directional, bringing a word of wisdom to address a specific problem or circumstance or decision in one's life.

Jacob's Business Dreams

Jacob received a divine word of wisdom through a dream as he contemplated taking his possessions and leaving the house of Laban. Many years before, when Jacob agreed to work for Laban, they had made an agreement concerning which of the flock were to be Jacob's—those of the flock which were streaked, speckled and spotted. This would give Jacob a fair portion of the flock for his salary.

But as time passed it was Jacob's portion of the flock which increased, and Laban grew jealous of Jacob's wealth. Laban dealt deceitfully with Jacob and changed his wages 10 different times over 20 years. Now as he sought to leave with his possessions and return to the land of his father, Jacob was anxious concerning how Laban would respond. So God sent a dream to Jacob at this time (during the breeding season) and gave him wisdom for dealing with this difficult situation:

> The angel of God said to me in the dream, "Jacob." I answered, "Here I am." And he said, "Look up and see that all the male goats mating with the flock are streaked, speckled or spotted, for I have seen all that Laban has been doing to you. . . . Now leave this land at once and go back to your native land" (Genesis 31:10-13, *NIV*).

This dream gave Jacob a plan of action for receiving the inheritance that God said was rightfully his and that Laban had tried to steal from him.

Later, when Laban heard that Jacob had left with his daughters and the flocks, he became very angry; but God sent a dream warning Laban not to do Jacob any harm or to even speak poorly of him (see Genesis 31:24). God protected Jacob's inheritance by instilling through the dream the fear of God in Laban.

Even as God desires to bless His people with their rightful inheritance, there will always be the Labans in this world who attempt to rob the blessing from the Church and the people of God. However, as we are sensitive to hear God's voice and receive wisdom from His throne, even through our dreams, He will show us how to take that which is rightfully ours without having to compromise our integrity in our business dealings. Jacob heard the voice of the Lord, and because he had allowed God's processes and dealings to be completed in his life, he was able to receive the blessing he had always sought.

Blessings in Business

A young man who works as a commodities broker called me one day to tell me of a dream he had a few weeks before. In the dream he went to his office and turned on his computer. As he looked at the screen, he saw the commodity symbol for coffee flashing, indicating a new high in the trading price. He specifically saw the number $1.44. Coffee was trading in the mid-80-cent range at the time he shared the dream with me.

We both commented on the prophetic nature of the dream and decided to simply watch to see what happened with the coffee market. Three weeks later, I received an excited phone call from the young man. He told me that when he turned to his computer screen that day, he saw the symbol for coffee flashing and the price of $1.44—just as his dream foretold! A freeze in South America had sent the price of coffee soaring. A minimal investment in one coffee futures contract at the time of his dream would have resulted in tens of thousands of dollars profit!

A word of caution before you invest your savings in pork bellies based on a dream: If you believe God has spoken to you about your personal future, it is always wise to submit the revelation to someone in a position of authority who can counsel you in your interpretation. *Never make a life-changing decision based solely on your own interpretation of a dream.* Rather, seek the confirmation of two or three who can provide mature counsel, for "in the multitude of counselors there is safety" (Proverbs 11:14).

We must remain watchful, even in our sleep, and listen carefully when the Lord speaks.

Many in the Church believe that in these latter days, God is causing the wealth of the wicked to be laid up for the just (see Proverbs 13:22; Deuteronomy 8:18). Just as Jesus sent Peter to go fishing and find the fish with the coin in its mouth so that they could pay the Temple tax (see Matthew 17:27), so the Lord may reveal divine opportunities for prosperity through supernatural revelation today. We must remain watchful, even in our sleep, and listen carefully when the

Lord speaks, that we might recognize the blessings He wants to release upon His Church.

Discerning of Spirits

Spiritual activity or specific insight into situations may be revealed through dreams to those who have the gift of discerning of spirits. It is important, however, not to assume that a specific person is evil or that you are "discerning" spirits just because you dream of some wrongdoing perpetrated by that individual. Your dream may have many other interpretations that would be more accurate. Many with a gift of discerning of spirits can fall prey to a critical spirit if they are not careful. Such gifts are given to edify the Body of Christ, not so that we may pass judgment.

That said, spiritual forces that may be influencing people or situations can be discerned through the insight of the Holy Spirit. Dreams may be one avenue by which this gift operates.

Poisoning of the Leader

I once dreamed that someone poisoned the leader of our ministry with the intent to kill him. He did not die in my dream but became very sick. As pastors of the church, my husband and I stood up to ask for special prayer on behalf of our leader. Before we could pray, however, someone came running up to me and whispered that we shouldn't announce what had happened because the person who had done the poisoning was right in our church. No one's name was mentioned.

When I awakened from the dream, I naturally felt concerned. I recorded the dream and began to pray about its meaning. I felt it may indicate that a spiritual attack was coming against not only the leader but also the ministry and that its intent was to bring death—not just physical death but also the death of the vision of the ministry. If I was correct, this death would result from a poisoning of minds and would be perpetuated from within the ministry. I asked the Lord to search my heart and show me anything therein that could be poisoning me.

Before 9:00 that morning, I received two phone calls. One was from one of our church intercessors who had been praying and felt that the Lord had showed him there was a spiritual infiltration in our church that was attempting to bring death. He specifically mentioned the name of our leader but felt that the whole church was being affected as well. The second phone call was similar, but this individual had had a dream that revealed a spirit of death coming against our church.

My dream and these two confirmations caused us to begin to pray as a church against the plans of the enemy. Since we don't wrestle against flesh and blood but against a spiritual foe, this is where the battle was won (see Ephesians 6:12).

The Spirit of Perizzites

On another occasion my husband and I were preparing to travel and minister in a series of churches. We had never been to any of these churches before, but the week before we left I had a dream. I saw us standing and preaching against the "spirit of the Perizzites" in the church we were to be in that Thursday night. (I was not even sure at the time where we would be on that night as another individual was scheduling our itinerary.) When I woke up, I wrote this down and went to look up the meaning of this name.

The Perizzites are mentioned in Genesis 15, Deuteronomy 7 and in the book of Joshua; this was one of the tribes that the children of Israel were told to drive out of Canaan. The name of this tribe meant "division" and "contention."

When we arrived at the church we were to minister in on Thursday, it became very evident that the church was full of division and contention. Even the leadership of the church was divided regarding the future direction of the church. We were able to encourage them to stand against the forces of darkness that had come to destroy them. God was so concerned over the situation in this church that He sent a dream to alert me as to what we would encounter.

The Gift of Faith

The gift of faith is a supernatural ability to believe and receive God's promises, even in the face of seemingly impossible circumstances.

My husband and I were believing God to provide us a new house. One night I dreamed that someone walked up to us and handed us a very large check and said, "Here, go and build your house." The amount on the check was very large and rather unusual in that it wasn't an even number. We were, needless to say, very excited.

When I awoke, I recorded the dream and the specific amount on the check in my journal. I shared the dream with my husband and we agreed in prayer to receive this blessing from the Lord.

Seven months went by as I waited expectantly for the fulfillment of this dream, but no one came forward to present us with a check. We felt led by the Lord to prepare to build the needed home by getting financing from a bank.

To our great disappointment, however, we did not have enough money to make the full down payment, so I asked the bank if they could make up the difference. I was told that they could not loan us any additional money. Yet I knew that, somehow, God was going to make a way.

The woman at the bank told me she would see if there was anything else she could do. I thanked her and hung up the phone. Fifteen minutes later, the bank officer called and told us they would not be able to loan us all we needed. However, they would be able to increase our loan amount. Then she named the amount. *It was exactly the same figure from my dream seven months earlier.*

The amount on our loan papers was the same figure written in my dream journal. The miracle was made complete by God whe He put the rest of the money we needed into our hands just days before we signed the papers.

This dream, with its specific amounts and fulfillment, brought tremendous faith and a supernatural ability to believe God to supply our every need.

This is one more example of how the Spirit's revelatory gifts may operate and function in our dreams. As you begin to exercise and use your spiritual gifts during your waking hours, these same gifts may produce the fruit of revelation generated by the Spirit of God while you sleep.

DREAMS, VISIONS AND SPIRITUAL WARFARE

For we do not wrestle against flesh and blood, but against principalities, against powers, against the rulers of the darkness of this age, against spiritual hosts of wickedness in the heavenly places.

EPHESIANS 6:12

In 2 Kings 6, we find the story of Elisha and his servant's being surrounded by the armies of Syria who sought to destroy the prophet. Every time they tried to move against Israel, the Syrians found that someone, presumably a spy, had exposed their plans. When they learned that the prophet Elisha was getting inside information concerning their strategies directly from the Lord, they sought him out, surrounded his camp and made plans to kill him.

Early that morning as Elisha and his servant awoke, they saw a great host of the enemy encamped about them. But Elisha wasn't troubled. His servant, on the other hand, was beginning to panic. Elisha calmly said to him, "Do not fear, for those who are with us are more than those who are with them" (2 Kings 6:16).

The servant must have looked at Elisha like he was *meshugga*. "What do you mean?!" he may have protested. "There are only two of us and thousands of them!" Elisha, however, knew what was *really* happening. God had given him the vision to perceive the situation from a heavenly perspective. So he prayed for his servant to be given that same vision:

> Elisha prayed, and said, "LORD, I pray, open his eyes that he may see." Then the LORD opened the eyes of the young man, and he saw. And behold, the mountain was full of horses and chariots of fire all around Elisha (2 Kings 6:17).

Just as the Lord had revealed to Elisha the battle plans of the King of Syria (see 2 Kings 6:8-12), enabling victory to come to the house of Israel, so God is disclosing to the modern Church the plans and tactics of our enemy, the devil, so that we may do battle and defeat our wicked foe. The Lord reveals such plans through prophecy, words of knowledge, words of wisdom and discerning of spirits. He sometimes chooses through dreams and visions to alert us to spiritual activity.

Occasionally, several people in our local church body (and sometimes people who live in other places) will be troubled by extremely similar dreams. Because of the disturbing nature of their dreams, these people may come to me as copastor of the church, only to discover that several others have had similar dreams within a short period of time. Many times these dreams will provide revelation concerning upcoming or ongoing spiritual warfare involving the local church.

Prayer is the key to properly responding to such dreams. In recent years, God has been raising up a worldwide army of intercessors—prayer warriors who are sensitive to our Supreme Commander's direction and are trained to do battle through prayer. These mighty warriors will call upon God for His divine intervention and angelic assistance, just as Daniel did when he battled a spiritual power known as the prince of Persia (see Daniel 10:13).

Many times the exposure through dreams of the enemy's plans will enable intercessors to pray for protection against natural disasters such as storms or earthquakes. Some have told of dreaming of destructive storms sweeping through their towns and leveling them flat. But when the foreseen storms actually hit, the prayers of the saints prevailed and damage was minimal.

We must not underestimate the power of prayer in dealing with the dark forces that have made plans against God's Church. Instead, we must arise with boldness and take our rightful authority given to us by Christ (see Luke 10:19). To be most effective, we must utilize every biblical means for obtaining divine insight into the heavenly realm, be it through prophecy, discerning of spirits, or dreams and visions.

On several occasions I have had very explicit dreams concerning demonic forces.

The Spirit of Death

I had been battling what I thought was a spirit of infirmity, manifesting one infection and sickness after another, when in a dream, a caped figure resembling a superhero character appeared before me and declared, "I am the Spirit of Death and I have come to take your life!" I was initially very frightened. Then, within the dream, the Spirit of God rose up boldly within me and confronted this demonic force. "Why are you telling me this?" I demanded. Then I saw this horrifying spirit begin to shrivel and cringe in fear. He looked back over his bony shoulder and I saw the finger of God pointing at him commanding him, "Tell her who you are!" God forced this demonic spirit that had been harassing me to reveal himself, so I could stand in the authority given me in Jesus' name and defeat this enemy. I woke and prayed and broke the power of the spirit of death. Soon afterward, I was strong and healthy again.

Warfare and Intercession

In one dream, I was flying through the air, binding hordes of demonic forces as the intercessors of our church walked on the ground and shined a huge flashlight on their hiding places. I recall being frightened in the dream, although I knew I had the power and ability to do what needed to be done. I remember dealing specifically with a witchcraft spirit that had been coming against our ministry.

When I awoke in the night, I sensed that there was in fact a spirit of witchcraft coming against us at that time. I turned to wake my husband, who was sleeping soundly. I touched him on the shoulder and quietly said, "Tom." Suddenly, he jumped out of bed and began rebuking evil spirits and commanding them to leave our house. I had not said a word to him about what I was sensing, yet he immediately knew what God was directing us to do. He startled me so much—if I wasn't fearful before, I certainly was then!

We began to pray and move through our house, rebuking the spirit of witchcraft. Our children were all lying on the floor instead of in their beds and were seemingly being tormented, for they were tossing and turning and wrestling in their sleep. Our oldest daughter came out of her room with a nosebleed, the blood running down her neck and arms. It was a frightening sight in light of what was happening. We continued to pray over our church and the churches connected with our ministry until we felt the spiritual attack had lifted.

Interestingly, we later heard from several others who had similar experiences at approximately the same time that night. God revealed through the dream what was happening and directed us to the warfare that needed to take place.

Again, it is important to carefully evaluate any dream involving demons or even angels. Do *not* continuously look for revelation concerning demonic activity through dreams and visions. To do so can leave us open to demonic influence and deception. But when God does stir you in a dream and directs you to pray, you should battle in faith—not fear—knowing that Christ has already won the victory for us. We must enforce that victory in our lives and on the earth through prayer.

Battle in faith—not fear—knowing that Christ has already won the victory for us.

Dreams and Deliverance

At times, God will use the revelation from a dream or vision to bring forth deliverance for an individual or a situation.

Earlier in her life, a woman had suffered from the bondage of anorexia—an eating disorder which causes in (mostly) women a desire to be extremely thin, which is achieved through starvation and sometimes frequent vomiting. The anorexic uses these extreme measures as a means to cleanse or purge herself and thus feel in control of her life. But this particular woman had received deliverance and healing from the Lord and was able to walk in freedom for many years.

Unfortunately, spiritual curses can be passed from one generation to the next because of the sins of our forefathers (see Exodus 34:6,7). Years later, this woman's teenage daughter began to experience the same difficulties and bondage. During a season of time when this woman was praying and fighting for her daughter's life, the Lord gave her a dream and showed her that her daughter was affected by a generational curse that had originated with her ancestors, Creek Indians.

In the dream this woman saw her Indian ancestors and rows of green corn. She decided to research the significance of this dream and found that the Creek Indians had held an annual Green Corn Ceremony in which they would eat green corn and then vomit it back up. They did this for three days as a form of cleansing and purging the soul. She realized that the disorder she and her daughter had struggled with was the result of a generational curse passed down their immediate ancestral line. She was able to pray for her daughter and bring forth deliverance by the Spirit of God, and today both mother and daughter are walking completely free of this bondage.

Chapter 12

THE LANGUAGE OF
SYMBOLISM

And [the butler and baker] said to [Joseph], "We each have had
a dream, and there is no interpreter of it." So Joseph said to them,
"Do not interpretations belong to God?"

GENESIS 40:8

In order to examine the messages contained in our dreams and visions, it is imperative that we begin to develop an understanding of symbolism. When a person dreams a dream or has a vision, he or she may have a clear picture of what God is trying to say because the revelation is very straightforward, needing few or no interpretive skills to bring understanding. In many cases, however, dreams and visions come to us in disjointed scenes, pictures and conversations that make little sense on their own.

Most dreams are communicated using people, places, things and activities that are symbolic of specific emotions, ideas, character traits and even events. This is where the language of symbolism comes in. Some people dream short, concise dreams, while others dream as though they are watching a feature-length movie. (Some people even report dreaming end credits!) The length of the dream does not matter—only what it contains and what those elements communicate.

Dr. Gayle Delaney, who spends a great deal of time studying dreams from a scientific perspective, says "Dreams are very much like poetry. You understand them if you get the metaphor." Understanding symbolism is essential to accurate dream interpretation.

Symbolism is the most basic and elementary language there is. Ancient cultures recorded their history using pictures and symbols. When traveling in a foreign land, you needn't fear finding yourself in the wrong restroom because those designated for either men or women are clearly indicated through the use of symbols. Every day we see road signs utilizing symbols to give information and direction. The reason for this is that symbols are a basic language and can be easily understood by anyone.

Unfortunately, any discussion of dream symbolism tends to intimidate people into thinking the symbols are too difficult or too complex to understand. As I mentioned previously, part of the reason for this is the prevailing attitude of our Western culture, which has a basic lack of patience when it comes to symbolism, whether in art or in dreams.

This is not so in the cultures of the Eastern world, of which the Jewish people are considered to be a part. Jesus never hesitated to speak to His disciples using the language of symbolism. On many occasions He related truths through the use of parables that were rich with symbolism. Sometimes He then interpreted the parables, since their meaning was veiled.

You may ask why Jesus didn't just say what He meant without concealing the meanings in symbols. This could be because there is a depth to symbolism that mere words do not have. Symbols give a broader meaning to what is being described.

John Sanford, a popular Christian author on the subject of dreams, describes it this way:

The Eastern courtesy of speaking indirectly is founded upon this principle, that each man retains best what he has discovered for himself. So God often prefers to speak indirectly. We may prefer to be like Thomas, who directly put his fingers in Jesus' side, but Jesus pronounced us more blessed who have believed not seeing directly (see John 20:29).[1]

Though symbols may take more effort to understand than words, it is well worth the effort to learn this fascinating language so that we might more fully comprehend God's messages to us.

God's Book of Symbols

Dream interpretation would be very easy if someone could write a book listing different symbols and their meanings, so when we have a dream we could simply plug in the appropriate symbols to arrive at a clear interpretation. Unfortunately, this does not work when trying to interpret dreams. Because symbolism is highly individualized according to the life experience of each person—and each person's own perception of his or her experiences—it is impossible to compile a comprehensive, authoritative book of symbols. Each symbol means something different to each person.

For example, a man who loves dogs may have a pleasant dream in which a dog appears in a room with him. For that individual the dog is a symbol with very specific personal connotations. But this dream would have an entirely different meaning if dreamed by someone who harbors a tremendous fear of dogs. The dog symbolizes different things to these two different people.

To one it may represent comfort, friendship or safety, while to the other it may represent fear, danger or a threatening situation.

Because dream images are taken from the individual's subconscious mind, the images will represent different things to different people.

The Bible should be the primary source one goes to for discerning the meaning of symbolism in dreams. The Word of God is rich with typology and symbolism and can often give a depth of understanding to images and pictures. Though you will not find every symbol's meaning in Scripture, it is often a big help in bringing clarity to what the Lord is saying. The Bible will also often give confirmation to the interpretation received.

At times it may be helpful to utilize other research materials when trying to discover the meaning of a particular symbol. A dictionary and an encyclopedia can often be useful tools when a symbol stands out in a dream but seems to have little relevance to the conscious mind.

Dual Meanings in Dreams

In discussing symbolism and its meaning, it is important to recognize that our dreams may often hold two meanings. These are often referred to as the primary and secondary meanings, or internal and external meanings.

A biblical example of the dual nature of many dreams is Nebuchadnezzar's dream as found in Daniel 2. The king of Babylon dreamed of an image with a head of gold, breasts and arms of silver, belly and thighs of brass, legs of iron and feet of iron and clay. Daniel interpreted the dream for the king, saying that God had revealed both the future as well as the present condition of the king's heart (see Daniel 2:28-30). And yet as he gave

the interpretation of the four kingdoms and the coming of the
Messiah, Daniel chose not to disclose directly that portion of the
dream's meaning which concerned
the king's spiritual state. God
would deal with the king's heart.

When considering prophetic
dreams concerning the future, the
lives of others or spiritual conditions of the heart, we must not neg-
lect to look beyond the primary
interpretation to what may lie
beneath the surface meaning. God
may in fact be revealing within the
same dream areas of our personal
lives that need to be dealt with.

For example, because we live in a
day of tremendous spiritual warfare,
it may be natural for me to perceive a
dream concerning a battlefield, a
war scene or other military setting as
indicative of a battle raging in the
heavenly places. While this may in
fact be a valid interpretation, there
may be further dealings of God's
Spirit relating to an inner battle or
conflict that my subconscious mind
or my spirit is struggling to resolve.
If we remain sensitive and open to
the deeper meaning of such dreams,
we will be better equipped to cooper-

Prayerfully consider

your dreams.

Do not miss their

meaning by settling

for a shallow

interpretation.

ate with God in becoming healed, whole individuals.

For this reason, when we dream of other people, we must allow the Holy Spirit to provide the proper interpretation. Is He is in fact showing us something prophetic regarding that person or is He telling us something about ourselves? In the dream I related earlier about chasing my son, he was flirting with dangerous situations and eventually fell through the ice of a frozen pond. Had I looked at the dream from a surface level, I may have supposed that God was showing me something regarding a dangerous circumstance ahead for my son. But this would not have been a proper interpretation to that dream, for God was trying to deal with my heart. If I hadn't carefully and prayerfully considered the dream, I might have entirely missed the message by settling for a shallow and improper interpretation.

Let me share with you another dream that illustrates this point.

The Unfaithful Family

A certain couple in our church was seldom consistent in their attendance. There were many reasons for this; however, I also knew there was some dissatisfaction that kept them from fully entering into fellowship. One night I had a dream in which someone had stolen their children. After some time, the thief returned them at the church and sped away. We were overjoyed that the children had been returned! But when we tried to contact the couple to let them know we had their precious children, we learned that the couple had changed their phone number and moved to a different house. We had no way to contact them and this was very frustrating.

When I awoke, I immediately felt this dream realistically described the situation with the couple and their sporadic attendance at the church. I believed that because of some kind of dissatisfaction, they had isolated themselves from the church. Thus when they needed us and we actually had the solution to their problem, we had no way of reaching them. I followed through soon after this dream, contacting the couple and encouraging them to stay involved and in touch so that as needs arose we would be able to help in whatever way we could. I did not share my dream with them but felt that I only needed to do what I could to keep them from being isolated.

I felt then that I had followed through on what the dream had revealed to me. A few months later, however, the Lord dealt with me regarding this dream.

"Jane, remember the dream about this couple?" He asked.

"Yes, Lord! They seem to be doing so much better since I had the opportunity to pray for them and encourage them."

"Jane, look at the dream again," the Lord directed me. "It wasn't only about them—it was also about you!"

As I prayed, the Lord revealed a very personal message in the dream. The couple represented that part of me that struggled with commitment and faithfulness, and the enemy came and stole my children—my blessings and inheritance from the Lord—because of it. As the couple in the dream had isolated themselves by changing their phone and residence, so I had isolated myself through a lack of sufficient communication through prayer and study of the Word. In the dream the thief returned the children, but because communication was cut off, the children could not be given to their rightful parents.

In my life, God had many stolen blessings to return to me; but I first had to reestablish a prayerful relationship with the One who held every solution to every problem I faced. God dealt with me about trying to handle my problems in my own strength and wisdom. This dream had a dual meaning and I was required to respond to both aspects of it.

Through dependence upon the Holy Spirit's guidance, I arrived at the proper interpretation. The ungodly also interpret their dreams, and they may often recognize the heart cry of their souls; but without God's influence they will miss the fullness of revelation to be derived from their dreams.

The Setting of Dreams

Because the symbols of dreams and visions come out of our subconscious minds stirred by the Spirit of God, it is natural for a dream to be set against the backdrop of our lives. Joseph interpreted two dreams, those of the Pharaoh's butler and his baker, in Genesis 40. On the surface these dreams seemed very similar in content; however, the correct interpretations were as different as life and death. The difference in their dreams was the setting of the lives in which they took place. When interpreting a dream, we must often examine what is happening in the life of the dreamer at the time of the dream in order to understand what the dream is really saying.

Dreams are not limited to addressing only a current situation, sin or difficulty. They may deal with a long-standing problem or even something from our past we have tried to forget. God knows all things, however, and may use a dream to bring to mind some unhealed hurt. Many of us struggle with insecurity or loss of identity or areas of hurt and unforgiveness. These places of pain will often surface during our sleep, when our natural defenses are down. Imbalances in our personalities may be identified and an appropriate resolution offered through the message of the dream. I had an interesting dream which clearly demonstrates this principle.

The College Girls

The dream was set on a college campus and involved three girls who were roommates. One of the girls was rich, one was poor, and one was from a middle-income family. The poor girl hated the rich girl. The rich girl had difficulty getting along with the poor girl. The girl in the middle was constantly trying to reconcile their differences. One day, the poor girl went to her boyfriend, a rough biker-type dressed in black, and asked him to help her kill the rich girl. The girl in the middle learned of the plot and called her father to intervene in the situation. That night, as the rich girl was walking across a bridge on her way home from class, the poor girl and her rough boyfriend stood in her path and began to disclose their murderous intentions. Suddenly, the girl in the middle appeared with her father and stepped between the attackers and the rich girl. The poor girl, realizing her folly, quickly repented of what she had almost done and told her boyfriend to stop. The boyfriend was determined, however, and proceeded to confront the father. The father wrestled with the attacker and eventually threw him over the side of the bridge into the icy waters below. He then gathered the three girls in his arms and told them they were actually all three his daughters who were separated at birth and now they were together again as a family.

I know this sounds like a bad melodramatic novel, but that was how the dream went, and the Lord used it to show me something about myself. The three girls represented different parts of me: the part that was spiritually rich, confident and secure; the part that was spiritually poor, easily caught up in emotions and susceptible to deception and evil doings; and the third part always trying to reconcile the other two.

At the time of the dream, I was undergoing intense emotional adjustments in my life in the ministry and as a young mother. I was experiencing frustration and stress and feelings of being pulled in several different directions.

The dream was set on a college campus, a place of learning. This confirmed that God had set me in a time of growth. When it appeared that the poor (sinful) girl was going to overcome and destroy the (spiritually) rich girl, the one in the middle who was trying to bring balance ran and got her father (God, the Father), who destroyed the attacker (the enemy of my soul, dressed in black). The poor girl had a change of heart and attitude and the end result was that God reconciled all three girls (all three parts of me) and they basically lived happily ever after. God was speaking to me of allowing Him to defend me and to bring balance to my life. This dream ministered tremendous peace to my soul during an otherwise difficult time.

Though there was actually more to the dream and further interpretation, this portion shows how God may use characters in a dream to represent different parts of an individual's life to help resolve difficulties within his or her soul. Knowledge of the circumstances in that person's life will aid in establishing the setting of the dream and help ensure proper interpretation. Without an understanding of the inner conflict I was facing, someone else would have found it difficult to arrive at a full interpretation of this dream.

A Glimpse of the Eternal

In Daniel 7, we find the record of Daniel's prophetic dream about four beasts and their destiny. It's a highly symbolic dream with great spiritual significance. If you haven't recently read this chapter, I would encourage you to do so. The first half of the chapter relates the dream; the second half covers Daniel's interpretation. After reading the details of the dream, I had a vague understanding of what the dream might possibly be saying; however, when the full interpretation was given, I realized that I had evaluated the dream based on my limited knowledge and not through the revelation of God's Spirit.

The dream troubled Daniel and he asked for clarity concerning the dream's meaning. The revelation was indeed about future events but not events that would take place in Daniel's life or times. The dream was a revelation regarding the end-time kingdoms of the world and the evil one who would arise. The dream also spoke of the judgment of God that would come and the dominion of God and His people as they ruled in an eternal kingdom. Daniel ends his account, saying:

> As for me, Daniel, my thoughts greatly troubled me, and my countenance changed; but I kept the matter in my heart (Daniel 7:28).

When we have dreams or visions of this nature, God intends to bring some sort of change in our lives. Sometimes a glimpse of eternity is what our spirits need to help us press on in our daily lives. Like Daniel, though, we should be careful about sharing these dreams openly, lest some would try to make doctrine out of them.

Note
1. John and Paula Sanford, *The Elijah Task* (Tulsa, OK: Victory House, 1977), p. 170.

BASIC SYMBOLS

Scripture is rich with symbolism. In fact, without a basic under-standing of some of the symbols used by biblical writers, much of the message conveyed by the Spirit of God would be lost on us. Jesus spent a good deal of His time teaching through the use of parables thick with symbolism.

In learning to understand your own personal language of symbols that appear in your dreams, you may find it helpful to first comprehend the symbolic nature of Scripture. Some sym-bols, for example, are used to characterize more than one person or object. For example, a lion is used to symbolically represent Christ, His saints and even Satan:

Behold, the Lion of the tribe of Judah . . . has prevailed to open the scroll (Revelation 5:5).

The righteous are bold as a lion (Proverbs 28:1).

Your adversary the devil walks about like a roaring lion, seeking whom he may devour (1 Peter 5:8).

Let's look at some examples of symbols used in Scripture. They may even help you to understand symbols from your own dreams.

Christ Is Symbolized As:

A Scepter	Numbers 24:17
Commander of an army	Joshua 5:14
A Warrior	Psalm 24:8
A Rose	Song of Solomon 2:1
A Sanctuary	Isaiah 8:14
A Foundation	Isaiah 28:16
A Servant	Isaiah 53:11
A Branch	Jeremiah 23:5
A Fountain	Zechariah 13:1
A Ruler	Matthew 2:6
A Physician	Matthew 9:2
A Bridegroom	Matthew 9:15
A King	Matthew 21:5
Bread	John 6:48
A Light	John 1:4
A Door	John 10:7
A Vine	John 15:2
A Judge	Acts 10:42
A Rock	1 Corinthians 10:4
The Head of a Body	Ephesians 5:23
A Cornerstone	1 Peter 2:6
A Shepherd	1 Peter 5:4
A Lion	Revelation 5:5
A Lamb	Revelation 5:6
Bright Morning Star	Revelation 22:16

The Saints Are Symbolized As:

Treasure	Exodus 19:5
The sun	Judges 5:31

Trees	Psalm 1:3
Deer	Psalm 42:1
Doves	Psalm 68:13
Sheep	Psalm 78:52
Eagles	Psalm 103:5
Lions	Proverbs 28:1
Lambs	Isaiah 40:11
The stars	Daniel 12:3
Jewels	Malachi 3:17
Salt	Matthew 5:13
Lights	Matthew 5:14
Babies	Matthew 11:25
Fish	Matthew 13:48
Children	Matthew 18:3
Servants	Matthew 25:21
Branches	John 15:2
Runners in a race	1 Corinthians 9:24
A Body	1 Corinthians 12:20
Soldiers	2 Timothy 2:3
Vessels	2 Timothy 2:20
Stones	1 Peter 2:5
The Bride of Christ	Revelation 21:2

The Holy Spirit Is Symbolized As:

Rain	Psalm 72:6
Fire	Matthew 3:11
A Dove	Matthew 3:16
Oil	Luke 10:34
Wind	John 3:8
Water	Revelation 22:17

Satan Is Symbolized As:

Lightning	Luke 10:18
A thief	John 10:10
A lion	1 Peter 5:8
Red dragon	Revelation 12:3
A serpent	Revelation 12:9

This list shows that Scripture is full of symbolism, and those who desire to glean truth from it must have a basic understanding of this veiled way of communicating.

Symbolism in the Parables

Matthew 13 records Jesus' parable of the wheat and the tares:

> The kingdom of heaven is like a man who sowed good seed in his field; but while men slept, his enemy came and sowed tares among the wheat and went his way. But when the grain had sprouted and produced a crop, then the tares also appeared. So the servants of the owner came and said to him, "Sir, did you not sow good seed in your field? How then does it have tares?" He said to them, "An enemy has done this." The servants said to him, "Do you want us then to go and gather them up?" But he said, "No, lest while you gather up the tares you also uproot the wheat with them. Let both grow together until the harvest, and at the time of harvest I will say to the reapers, 'First gather together the tares and bind them in bundles to burn them, but gather the wheat into my barn'" (Matthew 13:24-30).

In this particular chapter Jesus uses several different parables to illustrate the truths of the kingdom of God. The Kingdom is likened to a sower and his seed, a mustard seed, leaven, treasure hidden in a field, a merchant man seeking beautiful pearls and a net cast into the sea.

When the disciples came to Jesus and asked Him to explain the parable of the tares, He began to assign meaning to each of the symbols used in the story:

Symbol	Meaning
The sower	The Son of Man
The field	The world
The seed	Children of the Kingdom
The tares	Children of the wicked one
The enemy	The devil
The harvest	The end of the world
The reapers	The angels

After assigning meaning to each of the symbols, Jesus then put them together to give the disciples a full interpretation:

Therefore as the tares are gathered and burned in the fire, so it will be at the end of this age. The Son of Man will send out His angels, and they will gather out of His kingdom all things that offend, and those who practice lawlessness, and will cast them into the furnace of fire. There will be wailing and gnashing of teeth. Then the righteous will shine forth as the sun in the kingdom of their Father. He who has ears to hear, let him hear! (Matthew 13:40-43).

You will find it helpful when interpreting your dreams to use a similar method to the one Jesus used. First, make a list of symbols that appeared in a dream and assign meanings to them. Then put them all together to understand the full meaning of the dream. Of course, in order to reach an accurate interpretation, you must (1) be sensitive to the voice of God's Spirit and (2) know what the symbols in your dream mean to you.

Personal Symbols

Though I cannot provide you with a comprehensive book of symbols, I can give you certain guidelines for interpreting symbols which may help you to begin to understand your own personal dream language. The following are symbols that I relate to when interpreting my own dreams:

Houses

Jesus often used parables about houses to represent a person's life and personality. In Matthew 7, He speaks of the house built on the rock and the house built on the sand to distinguish between different foundations on which a person's life is built.

Quite often when I dream about a house, the house represents me. The Lord is showing me insight into my personal life. I look at the condition of the house on the outside and the inside and seek to determine what God is saying concerning my life.

You recall my dream about the house that looked wonderful in the front rooms yet had dark and dirty rooms locked away in the back. This was the basic condition of my soul at the time—immaculate on the outside but harboring hidden areas in need of God's all-powerful cleansing touch.

I have also experienced dreams in which I discovered a new door in my house. When I walked through the door, I discovered a whole new wing to my house. This type of dream speaks of new areas of my life that God is opening up, whether in my personality or my ministry, or gifts and talents that God is bringing forth that I may not have known existed.

During the time when we were building our home, I had dreams involving the home-building process. These dreams had varying interpretations, some on a purely natural level, since much of my time was occupied with building our house. But on a spiritual level, God used these dreams to speak to me of areas of my life and family that were in the process of being built up.

Houses may also signify a past time in our lives and something God desires to address from that period. For example, dreams of a childhood home may speak of something from that portion of our lives that God wants to address, enabling us to deal with a root of fear in our adult lives that was laid during our youth. Or such a dream may pinpoint a specific traumatic experience or hurt (directly or indirectly). Again, because dreams are symbolic, one must look past the seemingly obvious circumstances of the dream to look at what is being conveyed from a spiritual perspective.

As a young teenager I often dreamed of various neighborhood houses from my childhood. These dreams usually contained evil or frightening scenes, even though I remembered my childhood as happy and carefree and my visits with neighbors as anything but traumatic. It wasn't until years later that God opened a door in my mind and brought back the memories of a man in my neighborhood who made improper advances toward me. Once God had healed those traumatic memories and I began to investigate my dreams, I realized that God, through my subconscious memories, was dealing with deeply imbedded pain that my conscious mind had blocked out.

People

People who appear in your dreams may have several meanings. You may be dreaming prophetically about someone else, or God may be showing you a part of yourself. The latter should be investigated first before you assume the dream refers to someone else. Again, let me caution you that when dreaming about another individual whom you know, you must be extremely careful not to casually assume a surface interpretation.

For instance, should you dream that your spouse is being unfaithful to you, do not assume this is a confirmation of your suspicions. Rather, God may be dealing with your own insecurities and your need to establish trust in your marriage. Disturbing dreams about your boss or your pastor do not mean that you should not trust these people but may be dealing with your ability to submit to people in authority.

An example of this is a dream experienced by a young lady in our church. In her dream she was in a dentist's chair. A younger girl whom she had had some struggles with held the controls to the chair. The younger girl caused the chair to shoot up into the air, dumping the lady onto her head. The fall caused her not to be able to see straight, so it was hard to determine whether this was an accident or the young girl had done it on purpose.

Had the lady assumed a surface interpretation, she may have felt this young girl was going to try to manipulate her or cause her harm. Actually, after she inquired of the Lord, she believed the correct interpretation was that the young girl was representative of the immature part of her that she struggled with. This immature part of her was trying to control her and cause her harm, which would cause her to lose her vision and purpose. This was what the dream was revealing to her, and she considered it a warning from the Lord and an opportunity to develop maturity in a critical area of her life.

When dreaming of other people and determining what God may be saying about a part of your life, first look at the dominant personality trait of the individual or what that person symbolizes to you. How does that person make you feel? God may be using the image of this person to pinpoint a blind spot in your personality that needs adjustment.

For instance, if you dream about a friend who is pressuring you or manipulating you to do something you know is wrong, you should ask yourself *Is this something I do with my friends?* or *Is this an area in my life I need to be alerted to?* Then be sensitive to hear God's message. Listening to the Holy Spirit is the most important part of finding the true interpretation to any dream.

When in a dream a particular person frightens you or offends you, take a closer look at areas of your own life where you may be doing the same to others. As in my dream about my son, I was not actually dreaming about my child, but rather God was desiring to deal with the areas of my life which were young and immature before they could hinder my spiritual growth.

Through dreams about other people God may also try to bring balance into different aspects of our personalities. In each of us there exist characteristics and traits that we typically think of as being either masculine or feminine. For instance, we think of soft, tender, gentle, submissive traits as those belonging generally to women. Those traits which are typified as strong, intellectual and authoritative are considered to be masculine in nature. Dreams involving a mother or sister or grandmother might be addressing personal traits referred to as feminine, while dreams

Listening to the Holy Spirit is the most important part of finding the true interpretation to any dream.

involving a father, brother or other male family figures may deal with our more masculine traits.

When the dreamer is a female, God may challenge her to develop traits that include strength and determination, while God may challenge a man to get in touch with that side of himself which allows for displays of tenderness and sensitivity. Again, there are no set rules here and it is always best to inquire of the Lord to gain a full understanding of your dreams.

Crowds of People

A crowd of people in your dream may represent your concern with public opinion or feelings of peer pressure. Look closely at your dream response to the crowds. God may be dealing with a fear of man or a fear of going against the crowd. He may be challenging you to rise above the status quo and break forth into a new area of His calling.

Flying

When I fly in my dreams, I usually have to exert effort—flying doesn't come easily for me. However I am usually successful in flying after a time of effort in getting off the ground. I normally relate this act to a time of overcoming and the rewards afforded me from the victory. Overcoming often takes effort, thus my tendency to dream of having a bit of difficulty getting airborne. But once I overcome, I have a new, fresh perspective of my situation, which is the same with the sensation of flying in dreams.

Flying to new heights may speak of new ministries or giftings that God desires you to move into or new areas of freedom which God desires for you to experience. Flying has often taken me out of the grip of a would-be attacker in my dreams. The Word of God is rich with promises to those who overcome:

> But those who wait on the LORD shall renew their strength; they shall mount up with wings like eagles (Isaiah 40:31).

> And he who overcomes, and keeps My works until the end, to him I will give power over the nations (Revelation 2:26).

God often shows me areas to overcome and the benefit of overcoming through dreams involving flying.

Animals

The symbolism attached to different animals will come from each dreamer's personal experience, although some animals typically bring certain characteristics to mind. Snakes often make people fearful and may represent subtlety, trickery or danger. They may also represent wisdom, as in "wise as serpents" (see Matthew 10:16). Dreaming of a large animal such as an elephant or rhino or bull may be speaking of situations or emotions which you feel intimidated by, as though they could run you over and flatten you.

A good example of how the Lord uses animal symbols in dreams can be found in the book *Hippo in the Garden* by Pastor James Ryle of Boulder Valley Vineyard. In this book, Ryle tells of having a dream in which he saw a man lead a large hippopotamus into a garden. As he lay contemplating this dream after waking, the Lord impressed on Ryle that the hippo represented a "strange" thing He was getting ready to do in His Church. He likened the hippo to the prophetic movement, comparing several natural characteristics of the hippo to the prophet.

For example, the mouth of the hippo is one of its more distinctive characteristics, so it is interesting that God would choose this animal to represent His mouthpieces, the prophets. Ryle also notes that the hippo serves an important ecological function: in the riverbeds, it eats and stomps down weeds that would otherwise grow unimpeded until they choked off the flow of the river and caused the water to become stagnant. One of the purposes of prophetic ministry is to destroy in our lives the weeds that would choke off the flow of the river of God and cause our spiritual walk to become stagnant.[1]

Colors

Colors have always had a highly symbolic value, even in Western culture. Flags of different countries utilize colors based on the values of that particular land. The flag of the United States of America incorporates red, representing courage; white, representing purity; and blue, representing loyalty. Some of the symbolic colors mentioned in Scripture include red, white, green, blue, yellow, purple, scarlet, gold, silver and brass.

Red often symbolizes the blood of Christ, redemption and salvation, but red can also symbolize courage, anger ("I saw red") or fire. Blue is often a soothing color representing hope and healing; however the opposite can also be true. Having "the blues" speaks of being depressed or without hope. Yellow is generally a bright and cheerful color but can also represent lack of courage or fear. Green often symbolizes life, while white denotes holiness and purity. Purple has long been thought to represent royalty and majesty. Black quite often signifies evil or darkness.

Investigating the different qualities you assign to individual colors will give depth to the interpretation of certain elements of your dreams. A favorite color appearing in a dream will obviously hold different significance from dreaming of a color you do not care for.

Clothing

The clothes you are wearing in a dream may give insight into the message of the dream, especially if the clothes stand out as being either casual (comfortable) or formal (sophisticated or stiff). Many people have dreams of arriving at church, at school or at work in their underwear or even naked. While there are many different interpretations of this dream situation based on the current circumstances of the person's life, I usually relate such dreams to either a time of being unprepared or a fear of certain weaknesses or hidden matters being "exposed."

Money

Money may be prominent in some people's dreams based on a lack of money (or perceived lack) or an abundance. Money may signify a person's desire for security or power. Take a good look at the role money, finances or material prosperity plays in your dreams. As Jesus said, "Where your treasure is, there your heart will be also" (Matthew 6:21).

Death

Death or dying in dreams is usually not a foretelling of actual physical death but may speak of God's bringing death to the flesh in worldly areas of our lives. However, we must be open to God's use of death in dreams to reveal the evil intentions of the enemy so that we can respond in prayer and confound the enemy's plans. Death in a dream may also mean one is fearful or insecure, since the ultimate end of most fears lies in the fear of death. Such dreams may be spiritual, revealing things to our hearts; or they may be soulish in origin, mirroring our fears.

Pregnancy or Babies

Women (and at times even men) may dream of having a baby or being pregnant. Some may tend to interpret such dreams as confirmation of the impending birth of a natural child. However, these dreams may have a spiritual meaning, such as being pregnant with vision. Or the baby may represent something that God wants to birth in the dreamer's life or a situation that requires constant care and attention.

Numbers

Numbers are highly symbolic and rich in meaning. The following are the standard meanings of numbers according to biblical numerology:

Number	Meaning
One	Unity, God
Two	Agreement, witness
Three	The Trinity, Deity
Four	The earth (four winds, four corners)
Five	Grace, redemption, five-fold ministry
Six	Man
Seven	Perfection
Eight	New beginnings
Nine	Manifestation of the Spirit
Ten	Judgment
Eleven	Mercy
Twelve	Government of God
Thirteen	Double blessing, double cursing

Other Symbols in Dreams

The wide variety of symbols appearing in dreams prohibits a thorough discussion. Some other common symbols found in dreams may include:

Weather conditions such as storms, tornados, snow or even a bright sunny day could shed some light on the setting of the dream and give some indication of the message the dream is trying to communicate.

Vehicles in dreams may indicate how you as the dreamer feel in regard to being in control of certain situations in your life. For instance, are you driving the car, sitting in the passenger seat, or riding in the back seat with no control or influence whatsoever on where things are going? Are you riding a bike, making slow but steady progress? Are you riding this bike on a busy city street, leaving you feeling vulnerable? Are you riding a bus, possibly feeling pressured by a lot of people?

An interesting recurring theme in the dreams of several men I have spoken with is the *severing of fingers* from their hands. The hand is scripturally referred to as representing strength, power or control. God may be illuminating areas where these individuals feel they are losing power or control in their lives.

Whatever symbols appear in a dream, they must be either interpreted by the Holy Spirit or analyzed in light of the dreamer's experience and not solely by an interpretation imposed by another individual. Never impose your interpretation of a symbol on another if the dreamer does not bear witness to it. God will give the dreamer assurance and peace when the proper representation of the symbol is found.

Note
1. James Ryle, *Hippo in the Garden* (Guildford, Surrey, England: Highland Books, 1993), pp. 250-260.

Chapter 14

INTERPRETING YOUR DREAMS AND VISIONS

God desires to see the lives of His children transformed by His power and love, and He gives us every opportunity to make choices to become more conformed to the image of His Son. When He sends forth His Word, He intends for it to accomplish a purpose in the lives of those who receive it (see Isaiah 55:10,11; Romans 8:29).

Before one can respond to God's voice, however, it is important to be able to clearly and properly interpret what He is saying.

Whatever God is speaking to us, it is always in our best interest to follow His leading. He sees the end from the beginning, after all, and we can rest assured that that for which He is asking is for our own good and for the good of the Body of Christ.

When a dream comes to you and you recognize God's voice in the dream, you can be sure He will expect you to respond to what He is saying. Learning the art of interpretation and understanding what is being conveyed in your dreams are necessary before you can properly respond.

We have discussed at length the validity, purpose and language of dreams. Now we will look at the principles for interpreting dreams so that you may please God by properly responding.

Anointing for the
Interpretation of Dreams

Just as some are anointed to prophesy, so there are those who have a gift for interpreting dreams. Daniel and Joseph were prophets who were divinely gifted to interpret dreams. As a matter of fact, the main thrust of their prophetic ministries was interpreting dreams for national leaders. They were provided a forum for the word of the Lord to come forth and change the course of history.

Although dream interpretation is not one of the nine gifts of the Spirit, the prophetic nature of gleaning revelation from dreams may utilize some of these gifts. Those with a strong prophetic anointing often demonstrate a supernatural ability to discern the meaning of dreams.

Though not all those recognized as prophets are divinely gifted to flow in interpretation of dreams, many find that God has given them special insight in such matters. A prophet's interpretation will usually entail greater clarity and detail and will probably provide greater insight into the prophetic meaning behind the dream symbols. Those called to the office of prophet may also be more adept at uncovering the deeper instructional meanings of dreams.

Although most of us are not in the position of being prophets, many have a gift of prophecy (see 1 Corinthians 12:10) and may find that with practice they can become quite proficient at dream interpretation. Those interpreting their own dreams on this level can receive instruction and direction through dreams but should have someone in a position of leadership in their lives verify their interpretations before making any major life changes. Those operating in this gift will occasionally receive dreams which contain a word from the Lord for another individual. Again, proper oversight should be sought before sharing these dreams.

Of course, it does not necessarily take special gifts or abilities to move or minister under a spirit of prophecy, "for the testimony of Jesus is the spirit of prophecy" (Revelation 19:10). The only requirement is that we be yielded to the Holy Spirit. Just as any saint can operate in the spirit of prophecy, so can any saint participate in dream interpretation. By simply being sensitive to the Spirit of God and to the language of dream interpretation, anyone can begin to receive insight from his or her own dreams. As the dreamer learns to discern the voice of the Lord in his dreams, confidence will arise; truth can be applied; and lives can be changed.

Any level of interpreting requires not only the anointing of the Holy Spirit for clarity but also the Word of God to avoid error. Once you receive an interpretation, regardless of its content—correctional, directional or simply edifying—it is important that you measure the interpretation against the principles of God's written Word. All revelation, whether from prophecy or dream interpretation, must agree with and spring forth from the principles set forth in God's Word.

Steps to Interpreting Dreams and Visions

Whether you are a beginner or a veteran of dream interpretation, the following are some guidelines to employ when interpreting your revelations. It is wise not to begin to interpret the dreams or visions of others until you have established a workable knowledge of your own language of symbolism. As with Daniel and Joseph, God will gift certain individuals with the ability to divinely discern the interpretation of dreams and visions. If you do not feel that you are one of those individuals, do not despair. You too can learn to interpret your dreams and visions by remaining open to the guidance of the Holy Spirit and through diligently investigating what God reveals.

The following are some basic steps to follow that will aid you in interpreting your dreams and visions:

1. *Pray before you go to sleep* and ask the Lord to speak to you through your dreams. Sometimes, we do not have simply because we do not ask (see James 4:2). God desires to speak to His people. We must desire to hear what He is saying.

2. We must sleep *expecting to receive* a spiritual dream. Everyone dreams each night, and an expectance to receive a dream from the Lord raises our awareness upon waking to consider what has been dreamed. It is much the same as tuning a radio to receive the radio waves that are floating through the air. God is always broadcasting messages, but our ability to receive them depends on our spiritual receivers being turned on and tuned in to receive the messages He is sending.

3. *Write down dreams and visions* in as much detail as possible. This is often best accomplished by keeping a notebook and pencil on the bedside table for easy and immediate availability upon waking. Some find it easier to keep a tape recorder by their bed to record dreams in the night and write them down in the morning. Write the dream down as soon as possible, without trying to interpret as you go and without imposing meaning on the symbols at this point. Some find that it is easier to keep the dream fresh if one avoids turning on bright lights to record the dream in the middle of the night. Others I have spoken with find that it is best for them if they avoid turning on any lights at all. They record the dream on a large notepad without worrying about neatness and then rewrite the dream the next morning.

4. *Keep a journal* so that you can review your dreams and keep a record of what your dreams are saying. At times God will reveal His thoughts through a series of dreams, which will be easier to see as dreams are written down in one central location. I have had a series of dreams, each one occurring approximately one month apart, that communicated an ongoing message in a specific area of my life. Had I not been keeping a journal, I may have missed the full impact of what the Lord was showing me.

5. *Consider the circumstances* surrounding the dream or vision. What situations emotionally, physically or spiritually have you faced recently? Is there a question that you have been struggling with or a situation you have been trying to understand?

6. *Consider the main message* of the dream or vision. What is your initial feeling regarding the dream's interpretation? Is it a dream of warning or direction? Is God trying to show you something about yourself or another individual? (Again, if you feel the dream is prophetic about someone else, stay open to the possibility that the dream may have a dual meaning.) Record this information.

7. *Record the setting of the dream and list each object, character and detail* and begin to determine what each represents. If you are unsure about what a particular symbol represents but have several ideas, write them all down and allow the Lord to bring greater clarity as the interpretation begins to flow. When I interpret a dream, I normally make a list of prominent characters and write out what I feel each may symbolize. At times I will list several possible meanings for that symbol, eliminating the ones that do not apply as the dream's meaning comes forth.

8. *Remember, dreams and visions may be symbolic.* Look at prominent characters, objects and situations and see if the Lord would clarify their significance as to what they symbolize. This is a time to rely on hearing the voice of the Lord and receiving the guid-

ance of the Holy Spirit. If you do not receive clarification, do not press or impose an interpretation. It will come forth in God's time as you remain open to hear from Him on this subject.

9. Once an interpretation comes, be sure to *measure it by the Word of God*. Any revelation that does not agree with the written Word of God should be rejected, however logical or relevant the revelation may seem. If it passes this test, and you have responded in prayer, God may direct you to share it with a friend, counselor or pastor for confirmation or further insight. You will not need to do this with every dream; however, those which may confirm a directional change in your life should be validated in this manner: "By the mouth of two or three witnesses every word shall be established" (2 Corinthians 13:1).

10. *Respond* to your dream in whatever way God directs you. He may require repentance in an area of your life or obedience to go and do something such as to call or minister to someone else. Or perhaps He will simply direct you to pray. Whatever He says to you, do it!

Interpreting a Dream for the Church

Dreams and visions can be for the individual experiencing the revelation, or the revelation may be for someone else. Sometimes the revelation is for the local church or for the whole Body of Christ. As we have seen, dreams can foretell the destinies of entire nations. Since my husband and I pastor a church in which we emphasize hearing the voice of the Lord through the gifts of the Holy Spirit, I am frequently given written dreams and visions that relate to what God is doing in our church. I personally experience dreams and visions relating to our local body of believers on a regular basis.

Occasionally, I also receive words that are applicable to the entire Body of Christ. Allow me to share one of these with you and explain how I interpreted the dream.

The Burning Building Dream

In this dream, I was an executive in a very large office building. I was walking out to the parking garage one day and met my husband, Tom, who was also an executive in the building. We were not yet married in the dream. We walked to our cars four levels up on the parking deck. On the way up, we passed two scary-looking people. When we got to our parking level, we looked down and could see the lobby of our building in flames! Though we were concerned, the fire did not immediately threaten us. But then a nearby power box on the wall exploded and sent flames shooting throughout the parking level. We began to run from the fire. When we reached the end of our level and came up against a solid wall, Tom cut a hole in the wall and we lowered ourselves four stories to ground level. When we were safely on the ground, we heard a noise above us and looked up to see a baby in the flames near the hole on the fourth floor. Tom quickly covered himself in a special fireproof lotion and ran back into the building to save the baby. In the meantime, I confronted the scary-looking people who had apparently set fire to the building. I arrested them "in the name of Jesus." I was very nice to them and when one of them tried to escape, he changed his mind and said that he would go with me since I had been so kind to him. Tom and I took the baby and our two prisoners to the local jail and turned them over to the warden. While leaving the station, we decided to get married and adopt the baby.

In interpreting this dream, which I knew the Lord had given to me, I had to first determine what the setting of the dream indicated and what the different symbols meant. I began by inquiring of the Lord to direct me in my interpretation. Sometimes I have an immediate understanding of the meaning of a dream and its symbolism; at other times it is a process of seeking God, contemplating the symbols and doing research if necessary.

In this instance I made a list of the setting, the people and the symbols. Then I prayerfully considered each one, filling in the blanks as I received clarity from the Lord. My final list was as follows:

- The building is the Church, the corporate Body of Christ. As Tom and I are pastors, the office building represented where we worked.
- Tom and I not being married yet represents Church members and leaders not yet unified.
- The people of questionable character are lost souls. And we walked right by them.
- Going up four levels means that God is bringing the Church and its leaders up to a new level. The number four is representative of the earth and restoration.
- The lobby is in flames! The Church is on fire! Many in America have been praying that the Lord would send His fire on the Church. Prophetic words have been coming with regularity concerning God's sending His fire. In Scripture, fire represents three things: (1) judgment (see 2 Thessalonians 1:8); (2) purification (see

1 Corinthians 3:13); (3) the presence and power of God (see Acts 2:4; Hebrews 12:29).

- The exploding power box is the power of God exploding on this new level.
- We ran from the fire. Many church leaders are afraid of the fire. Fearing it will destroy them, they run from it rather than embrace it.
- We escaped down four levels. Again, four represents the earth, the world. The fire of God is driving the churches beyond their walls and into the world.
- The baby in the fire represents the new restorational move of God's Spirit, birthed out of the fire!
- Just as Tom rescued the baby, Church leaders and members must face the flames in order to embrace the new birthing of God's Spirit.
- Tom's covering himself with lotion is representative of the anointing. We must be covered with the anointing of the Spirit to receive divine protection from holy flames.
- The scary-looking people who set the fire are persecutors of the Church—lost souls. They thought they were bringing destruction upon the Church, but instead new life was birthed. God may use the heathen and worldly circumstances to bring fire to our lives.
- I arrested the bad guys. They were captured by the Church. Spiritual authority was utilized in the name of Jesus to take dominion over the enemy, his plans and his cohorts.
- We were nice to them. These lost souls, however evil their intentions, were won over by our kindness and our love.
- We took the criminals to the warden. We brought them to the Lord.

- Tom and I were married. The Church, its leaders and members were unified because of the experience with the fire.
- We adopted the baby. The new move birthed by God out of the flames is embraced by all.

Interpreting this dream took time. It was a process in which I invested a great deal of prayer and meditation over a period of several days. What I learned was that God was showing me His plan for His Church and His purpose for sending the fire. He was assuring me that good things will come as Church leaders embrace the new move of God which will be birthed out of the fire. The Holy Spirit is surely on the move and new, exciting and challenging days are ahead!

Chapter 15

RESPONDING TO YOUR DREAMS AND VISIONS

That the God of our Lord Jesus Christ, the Father of glory, may give to you the spirit of wisdom and revelation.

EPHESIANS 1:17

When God spoke to a man or woman in Scripture, He required a response. When He told Adam not to eat of the Tree of Knowledge of Good and Evil, He expected obedience. When He told Noah to build a boat, that is just what He expected Noah to do. When He told Peter to go to the Gentiles, God expected Peter to lay aside his traditional mind-set and go minister the truths of salvation to those who were not of Jewish descent.

When God speaks today through His written Word, His desire is that His people follow after the truth. When He speaks through His prophets or through someone ministering out of the gifts of the Holy Spirit, that word should be judged and confirmed and then heeded. When He speaks to you in that still, small voice, God requires some corresponding action to that which has been spoken. He may want you to pray about something, to meditate on a particular verse, to go forth and perform some service, or to simply be still and know that He is God.

So it is when God speaks to you through a dream or vision. He not only desires to communicate something to you for your own information, but He also expects you to respond appropriately to whatever He has said. James 1:22 tells us, "Be doers of the word, and not hearers only."

Therefore, when seeking the Lord for a proper dream interpretation, one should also ask, "Lord, how would You have me to respond to what You have said?"

Personal Responses

He has sent Me to heal the brokenhearted, to proclaim liberty to the captives . . . to set at liberty those who are oppressed (Luke 4:18).

Because most dreams received from God deal with a personal area of one's life, it is vital that we respond by addressing any area God may have pinpointed. Many personal dreams are not to be shared with anyone else but are between God and the dreamer. God will often desire to move in one's life through bringing about repentance, deliverance or healing in many areas of the soul. But God does not do these works on His own; rather, He requires our cooperation to touch and change our lives.

Sin

There may be areas of sin that we will have to put away or areas of the flesh which we will be called upon to deny and crucify. When an area of sin is revealed to you in a dream, confess it to your Father, repent of that sin and receive the freedom that comes with forgiveness (see 1 John 1:9).

Hurts

God will sometimes reveal an area of emotional hurt or hidden memories through a dream. The natural mind may deny or suppress memories that are unpleasant to deal with, but the subconscious mind stores this information. Some dreams of this nature will be soulful in origin as natural memories and hurts surface. God may nevertheless use such dreams to deal with these areas. He will choose the time for these things to come to light, so He can touch these areas with His love and healing. Fearful dreams may actually be revealing a time of past pain. Remember, God is the healer of the brokenhearted (see Psalm 147:3)!

Oppression

Soulish concerns and anxieties as well as demonic oppression may be uncovered through the revelation of a dream or vision. Jesus' sacrifice on Calvary provided healing for our souls and gave His followers the authority to deal with every demonic foe: "Behold, I give you the authority to trample on serpents and scorpions, and over all the power of the enemy, and nothing shall by any means hurt you" (Luke 10:19).

When areas of oppression are revealed, we can stand and take the authority which has been given us by Christ and win the victory over every enemy of the soul. Do not hesitate to have others pray with you, as there is always strength in joining in prayer with another believer .

Mind-Sets

"You shall know the truth, and the truth shall make you free" (John 8:32). Dreams have a way of exposing ungodly beliefs or mind-sets. When a wrong mind-set is discovered or an ungodly belief exposed, we must allow the truth of God's Word to supplant the lie and begin the process of renewing our minds (see Romans 12:2). It often helps to write out the wrong belief and apply the Word of God by writing a Scripture verse which tells of the proper principle by which we should live and the attitude we should have.

Prophetic Responses

God may speak to you prophetically through dreams about your life, about others or about upcoming events from individual lives, the life of a church body or even the life of the world.

Warnings

Should you receive a dream of warning, either about yourself or about others, your first priority is always to PRAY! There is no substitute for responding to revelation with prayer. Then you may examine your life and actions to see if there is anything in your life which you need to change. Nebuchadnezzar's dream was one of warning requiring him to make some drastic changes in his life. Had he heeded the warnings he would have been spared much heartache.

Insight for Self

Anytime an individual feels that God has spoken a directive word to him or her—whether through a dream, a vision, a prophetic word or through study of the Word of God—there are certain safeguards to be observed in order to properly respond to the revelation. Dr. Bill Hamon's book *Prophets and Personal*

Prophecy lists three steps for properly determining the direction of the Lord. These steps are (1) the *word*, (2) the *will* and (3) the *way*. These may be helpful in learning the proper response to the personal interpretation of your dreams.

The first step that one must take to determine the will of God is to go to the Word. You must first determine whether or not the direction you are feeling is scriptural in nature. For example, should you feel that your revelation is directing you to divorce your spouse and marry another person, you should be able to easily and clearly determine from Scripture that this is not in fact a revelation from God, nor is it the will of God.

If you cannot ascertain whether the revelation you have received is biblically based, it is extremely dangerous to proceed further in responding to it as God *never* directs anyone to do anything contrary to His Word. The Bible is the standard measurement by which all revelation should be judged.

Consider whether or not following the message of this revelation will cause you to lie, cheat or

God *never* directs anyone to do anything contrary to His Word.

injure someone. If so, the direction is contrary to the principles of God's Word and it is probable that you have derived an inaccurate interpretation.

Once you have determined that the revelation is scriptural, you are ready for the next step: determining whether or not the revelation is in line with God's will for your life. There is the will of God which tells us to "go into all the world and preach the gospel" (Mark 16:15), but the specific will of God for an individual may be to go to a foreign nation, or to share the gospel with some people he works with or in his neighborhood, or maybe even to be involved in a prayer group to pray for those on the front line of spiritual battle.

Determining God's specific will for your life may include receiving confirmations such as having a God-given desire to do something, having specific Scripture verses illuminated by the Holy Spirit, receiving prophetic words from others, having a witness of the Spirit and receiving godly counsel.

If you have received green lights in each of these first two areas, you are then ready to proceed to the third step: determining the way God has made for you to accomplish what He has set for you to do. This will include such details as the proper timing, how to do it, whom you are to work with, the means that will be provided for you to do it, etc. Many people make the mistake of moving forward ahead of God's plans and perfect timing He has set for them. Once you have clearance to proceed in His will, you will be on your way to fulfilling the purpose of God in this specific area of your life.

Insight for Others
This is the area where people tend to make the most mistakes in responding to their dreams. While God does in fact sometimes

give us dreams regarding others, it is imperative that we use extra caution and wisdom when responding to such dreams. As we have seen, many times when you dream of other people, you may not be receiving a revelation or message for them; instead you may be actually dreaming about a part of yourself.

A dream about someone else that has no tangible relation to the dreamer but is merely prophetic in nature is somewhat rare. Those who are prophetically gifted—often intercessors or someone in a position of authority within the local church—seem to experience this type of dream more often than those who are not, perhaps because they are trained or tuned to God's ways of speaking or because they are in a position to address the circumstances being revealed.

Through dreams, I have often been made aware of church members who were experiencing sadness, distress or confusion. As a pastor of our church, I would casually call on these people the next day and often find them in the emotional state revealed in my dream. I was then able to encourage them that God knew what was happening in their lives and was alerting others to pray in their behalf.

If you have had a dream you believe is prophetic concerning another person, it is important that you proceed with caution. First, measure your interpretation by the Word of God to ensure it does not conflict; then take it to the Lord in prayer. God may have given you insight into an area of another's life for the sole purpose of praying for that individual to draw closer to Him. Sometimes prayer can alter disturbing events or even prevent them from happening. I have at times had a dream about someone and awakened with such an urgency to pray that I was sure God was intervening in that person's life at that very moment.

A serious word of warning: Be careful not to impose on others your dreams about them, particularly if you sense that their weaknesses have been exposed or that God has shown you some direction they need to take. This is equivalent to a corrective or directive prophetic word and should only be given to that individual with the proper consent and covering of established leadership. This protects the person sharing the dream from giving a wrong interpretation or perhaps even having the interpretation misunderstood.

Before you share your dream with that person who is the subject of the dream, it is always wise for you to go to someone in leadership who can give oversight and determine if the dream should be shared at all and if so, how it should be shared and when. Sometimes God does not intend for a dream or vision to be shared with anyone but only that prayer be offered up on another's behalf. You can always pray for the individual that God's plan will be fulfilled in his or her life—the prayer that never fails.

Unless you are seeking counsel from leadership concerning your dream, never share your dream about someone else with others. To share such subjective material as a dream with others who are not concerned in the matter could put you in a position of gossiping about or even slandering the one of whom you dreamed. First of all, you may not have the proper interpretation at all. And God never reveals something to expose another individual in a harmful way. Gossip is a destructive force that God will not abide (see 2 Corinthians 12:20).

The end result of any action you take should always be that the individual and the church body are edified.

Spiritual Insight

Prophetic dreams dealing with principalities and powers and activity in the spirit realm also should be addressed in prayer. God may require a time of fasting and prayer and spiritual warfare to deal with certain strongholds that have been discerned. From my own experiences with spiritual warfare, I recommend that you not get too deeply involved on your own; whenever possible, share the warfare with intercessors under the proper covering of leadership. The enemy loves to see us off doing our own thing—even good things like intercessory prayer—so that he might be able to separate us and destroy us.

Every individual who has been cleansed by the blood of Jesus and filled with the Holy Spirit and who has a working knowledge of the Word of God, has been given power over all the works of the devil. However, the Bible clearly talks about the purpose and value of joining with others in spiritual warfare. Deuteronomy 32:30 tells us that one shall chase a thousand, and two shall put ten thousand to flight. This represents an increase of 10 times the power to the force of our warfare!

Therefore, should you receive a dream requiring spiritual warfare, do pray and intercede; but do not forsake the strength God has provided when we join with others in unified prayer.

Prophetic Protocol

In most situations involving a dream of this nature, it is wise to present the dream to an elder or pastor if you believe the dream contains a message that may constitute a prophetic word or a word of direction. As with prophecy, that which is shared should bring edification, exhortation and comfort (see 1 Corinthians 14:3). The eldership may or may not feel that it would be appropriate to share the dream with the individual you have dreamed about.

If those you have submitted the dream to feel you should share the dream, it is always a good idea to have another person present, preferably someone in leadership, in order to avoid any misunderstanding that may arise.

If your dream contains a word for a church leader, you will find that your dream will be received with greater enthusiasm if it is submitted with a spirit of humility—without haughtiness, judgment or accusation. I know of instances when a dream has been thrown down like a gauntlet on a pastor's desk, with an attitude of pride and self-justification. Clearly, this is not the submission of Christ, nor is it the attitude with which we are to approach one another, let alone a spiritual leader.

These simple guidelines should help ensure that when you receive a dream, interpret it and follow through by responding to the message of the dream, you are doing so in accordance with biblical standards and wisdom. This will protect you and others as you endeavor to follow the will of God with proper oversight, accountability and counsel.

Happy is the man who finds wisdom, and the man who gains understanding; for her proceeds are better than the profits of silver, and her gain than fine gold (Proverbs 3:13,14).

Chapter 16

A CHARGE TO DREAMERS

Some are supernaturally gifted by God with the ability to interpret dreams and visions, just as some are gifted to prophesy. But for most of us, learning the art of interpretation will take time and will likely involve some trial and error.

Do not become discouraged, but remain patient as you learn to discern the voice of the Lord in your dreams and visions. Take the time necessary to develop a personal understanding of symbolism and how to properly respond to revelation. The rewards to your soul and spirit will be great as God visits you with new insight, illumination, inspiration and comfort.

Dreams can be activated by faith, just as Daniel was certain the Lord would enable him to tell King Nebuchadnezzar his dream and its interpretation (see Daniel 2:19). Likewise, visions can be activated by praying and asking God to open our eyes, just as Elisha prayed that his servant's eyes would be opened (see 2 Kings 6:17).

Once God's people learn to discern the voice of God in dreams and visions, we will begin to see even greater manifestations of God's power in the earth. Dreams brought promotion to godly, prophetic people such as Joseph and Daniel. Dream interpretations brought these godly, prophetic people into the presence of kings and enabled them to deliver messages that changed nations.

God has promised to pour out His Spirit upon all flesh in these last days. Sons and daughters shall prophesy, old men shall dream dreams, and young men shall see visions. God is no respecter of persons. Be sure that you are receiving your full portion of prophetic dreams and visions in these last days (see Acts 2:17,18).

God is challenging us to hear His voice and to receive a fresh impartation of the outpouring of His Spirit. He that has ears to hear, let him hear! (see Revelation 2:7).

> That the God of our Lord Jesus Christ, the Father of glory, may give to you the spirit of wisdom and revelation in the knowledge of Him, the eyes of your understanding being enlightened; that you may know what is the hope of His calling, what are the riches of the glory of His inheritance in the saints, and what is the exceeding greatness of His power toward us who believe, according to the working of His mighty power (Ephesians 1:17-19).

Sweet Dreams!

RECOMMENDED READING ON DREAMS, VISIONS AND PROPHECY

Hamon, Bill. *Prophets and Personal Prophecy*. Shippensburg, PA: Destiny Image, 1987.

———. *Prophets and the Prophetic Movement*. Shippensburg, PA: Destiny Image, 1990.

———. *Prophets, Pitfalls and Principles*. Shippensburg, PA: Destiny Image, 1991.

Jacobs, Cindy. *The Voice of God*. Ventura, CA: Regal Books, 1995.

Riffel, Herman. *Your Dreams: God's Neglected Gift*. New York: Ballantine Books, 1981.

Ryle, James. *A Dream Come True*. Orlando, FL: Creation House, 1996.

———. *The Hippo in the Garden*. Woodbridge Meadows, Guildford, Surrey, England: Highland Books, 1993.

Sanford, John. *The Elijah Task*. Plainfield, NJ: Logos International, 1977.

Thomas, Benny. *Exploring the World of Dreams*. Springdale, PA: Whitaker House, 1990.

RESOURCES BY JANE HAMON

BOOKS

The Deborah Company

Envisioning a new generation of women to arise and fulfill their destiny in the twenty-first-century Church. $10.00

AUDIOTAPES

Dreams and Visions

An exciting four-tape series on how God speaks through dreams and visions today. $20.00

Having a Discerning Heart

A four-tape teaching series on spiritual discernment and the gift of discerning of spirits. $15.00

Conquering the "Ites"

A four-part study of the seven enemy nations Israel was commanded to drive out of Canaan. Learn the meaning of the names of each of the "Ites" and how these nations represent those things that today try to prevent you from possessing your promised land. $20.00

Women of Destiny

A six-part series designed to inspire and challenge those who desire to be women of significance, purpose, destiny and power. $30.00

Releasing the Miraculous

A three-tape series on how to activate and release the miracle working power of God in and through your life and in the Church. $15.00

The Cyrus Anointing
A modern look at Cyrus the Great—the subject of a prophecy in Isaiah 45—as a type of the apostolic and prophetic Church arising on the earth today. Here are keys for unlocking hidden treasures and impacting the kingdoms of this world. $10.00

Understanding Serpent Spirits
A two-part series investigating the characteristics and workings of the Python and Leviathan spirits. Vital information for prayer warriors. $10.00

The Roots of Jezebel
A two-part series on the spirit of the Queen of Heaven and the Jezebel spirit. Understand the global significance of the operation of these demonic forces. $10.00

The Workings of Absalom, Antichrist and Behemoth Spirits
Three tapes designed to enlighten and empower the Church for battle against these destructive spirits. $15.00

Releasing the Double Portion
In this four-tape series, Tom and Jane Hamon challenge the twenty-first-century Church to step into the miracle anointing of Elisha—the double portion! $20.00

The Spirit of Excellence
Tom and Jane Hamon call the Church to walk in the spirit of excellence—the same heart and spirit of David and Daniel. $10.00

To order, write or call:
CHRISTIAN INTERNATIONAL FAMILY CHURCH
5200 East Highway 98, Santa Rosa Beach, FL 32459
(850) 231-2660